MW00909830

Effective CD Counseling

Early stage chemical dependency
counseling

S. Ed Hale

Effective CD Counseling

Early stage chemical dependency counseling

by

S. Ed Hale

WALDENHOUSE
WALDEN, TENNESSEE

About the cover: A typical group counseling session in a relaxed setting was simulated for this 1981 photo-illustration© by John W. Coniglio.

Effective CD Counseling:
Early stage chemical dependency counseling

© Copyright 2005, S. Edmund Hale   All rights reserved. The reproduction or use of this work, except for use in a review or in the exception stated below, in any form or by any electronic, mechanical or other means now known or hereafter invented, including photocopying and recording, or placed in any information storage or retrieval system, is forbidden without the written permission of the author or his legal representative. These rights may be transferred to a publisher or distributor at the discretion of the author. Materials designated as The Appendix may be photocopied or transcribed for the specific use in the education or training of clients or counselors. Materials may not be copied for sale, advertising purposes or publication without the written permission of the copyrighter. S. E. Hale, 6578 Hickory Meadow Drive, Chattanooga, TN 37421.

Published by Waldenhouse Publishers, Inc.
100 Clegg Street, Walden (Signal Mt.), TN 37377
423-886-2721 888-222-8228
www.waldenhouse.com
Printed in The United States of America

Library of Congress Cataloging-in-Publication Data

Hale, S. Ed. (S. Edmund), 1919-
  Effective CD counseling : early stage chemical dependency counseling / by S. Ed Hale.
     p. cm.
  Summary: "CD(Chemical Dependency) is a primary progressive illness in onset upon use of psychoactive substances by susceptible individuals. Recovery requires abstinence and relapse prevention. Effective CD Counseling describes recovery tasks and counseling techniques. Their rationales are explained for counselors and others"--Provided by publisher.
  Includes bibliographical references and index.
  ISBN-13: 978-0-9761033-3-2 (alk. paper)
  ISBN-10: 0-9761033-3-8 (alk. paper)
  1. Substance abuse--Patients--Counseling of. 2. Substance abuse--Treatment--Planning. I. Title.
  RC564.H33 2005
  362.29'186--dc22
                                        2005024422

Contents

Introduction: vii.

Chapter I: The Nature of Chemical Dependence   11

Charter II: Treating Chemical Dependence   17

Chapter III: Assessment and Diagnosis   25

Chapter IV: Collecting and Using Assessment Data   37

Chapter V: Progression in the CD Disease   57

Chapter VI: Relationship of CD Counseling to
     CD Recovery   71

Chapter VII: Abstinence in CD Treatment
     and Recovery   85

Chapter VIII: The "Sheep Dip" Presumption   95

Chapter IX: Change   99

Chapter X: Guidelines for Chemical Dependence
     Treatment   119

Chapter XI: On CD Treatment Goals   129

Chapter XII: The Power of Listening and
     Other Counseling Skills   145

Appendix: Listing of Appendices   169

Bibliography: An Annotated Bibliography   213

Introduction

Effective chemical dependency recovery must rely on the foundation of total chemical substance abstinence. Without this firm requirement, treatment efforts are ineffective and recovery is less likely if at all. As will be explained, this does not mean that the goal of treatment is just abstinence. The goal of CD treatment is to lay the foundation of change that will lead to life-long recovery as painlessly as possible. Effective chemical dependency counseling requires a recognition of the progressiveness of the CD disease in both its onset and its recovery. Effectively applied and seriously accepted, stage one CD treatment is relatively brief. An end goal of CD treatment is the preparedness of the client to be in charge of his own life-long recovery.

The goal of this brief book is to give the CD counselor a framework that has proven to prepare the client for a solid recovery. The reader will be aware that the Chemical Dependency Counseling approach and methods emphasizes the recognition of CD as a disease of biochemical and neurological susceptibility to psychoactive substances which cannot be corrected. The CD is in the same boat with the diabetics, those with high blood pressure, asthmatics and many other incurable health problems. While incurable, CD can be managed to the level of normal physical, social and psychological health. The outcome of CD management success is the result of making life changes and becoming personally responsible for his own final recovery.

Experienced CD counselors will recognize that many areas of chemical dependence knowledge have been given little or no attention. This was deliberate, first to keep the content as brief as possible and secondly confidence that these ignored subjects are already known to the reader and are probably in no way contradictory to the ideas presented.

An important subject not given adequate and deserved attention to regards counselor self-care. CD counseling has the reputation of being a fast turnover occupation. It is easy to become emotionally enmeshed in our clients' pains and struggles, and allow ourselves to slip unawares into a rescuer, persecutor or victim relationship with him. When that occurs, the counselor's effectiveness is drastically compromised and even troubles ensue. It is a difficult but necessary task to be the caring and attentive counselor while at the same time keeping the emotional and social relationships at a professional arms-length. For the counselor's emotional well-being and professional integrity, it must be done. After all, the counselor is important, too.

The myriad nuances of human personality, and its skewing by environment and human interactions, make impossible the effective application of a purely formalized or routine treatment approach. For that reason the Stage I treatment aims or tasks offered here are presented in a generalized way but should be applied in a very individualized manner. Given adequate time for tasks to be absorbed and presented with creative and thorough attention will result in a maximum of recovery progress in the shortest time. The full use of all tasks needed for a solid state of abstinence will be influenced by the client's environment and behavior-change capability.

An intent of this book is to focus and expand upon specific important areas of the CD counseling process. In addition to the importance of adhering to the principles of the progressiveness of the recovery, is an awareness that stage I treatment is perhaps the most critical of recovery phases. Initial assessment and treatment commitment are foundations of treatment effectiveness. Abstinence and a related life style are number one recovery priorities. Life style and related behavior changes are central to early and future recovery phases. Effective CD counseling must be client-focused. The client must be responsible for his own recovery, and deviations from these and related processes of change detract from the tasks of solidifying long-term sobriety.

Thanks for reading this book. It is sincerely wished that you will find something useful herein that will enhance your skills or add a few more CD counseling tools for your use.

SEH

Chapter 1

THE NATURE OF CHEMICAL DEPENDENCE

The recognition of alcoholism or other drug addiction in an individual can be obvious in many ways. Alcoholics and drug addicts do things that may be usual with persons with a mental illness or who are just naive or undisciplined. Oddly enough many chemically dependent people would accept one of these unwanted labels rather than to recognize their dependence on a chemical substance. Signs of chemical dependence are numerous: frequent intoxication, DUI arrests, lying about or hiding use, loss of dependability, frequent accidents, loss of jobs, disrupted relationships, neglect of responsibilities, or any number of other behaviors that are irrational or destructive to self or others.

In addition to recognition of the history of the irrational behaviors, two other areas of information must be known: evidence that the problem behaviors are related to alcohol or other drug use, and that behavior prior to alcohol or drug use was rational and responsible or otherwise sensible. A diagnosis of chemical dependence (CD), or Substance Dependence as the American Psychiatric Association calls it, does not require that the person also have a history of mental illness or criminal behavior.

A non-addicted person is said to be "under the influence" only when some degree of abnormal thinking, feeling or behaving is due to the current presence in the system of a psychoactive substance or is being affected by the lingering effect of very recent use. The addicted person may also be said to be legally under the influence in the same manner. However, in a different context the chemically dependent/addicted individual is under the influence of the illness whether or not he is currently using. For the addicted person it means having lost a significant degree of the ability to choose when or whether to use or not to use the psychoactive substance of choice. It further means an unrelenting compulsion to think about, plan for, use and recover from episodes of drug use, all of which colors the thinking, feeling and behaviors of every aspect of the person's life, whether using or not using at the time. The addiction has become central in the person's life. He does not rule it. It rules him.

Any discussion of how chemical dependence may be treated should be prefaced by an understanding of what chemical dependence is. It is presumed that most of the readers of this book may have some special interest in and some beliefs about what CD is and how it may be successfully treated. It has been only in very recent times that many workers in the field are comfortable in changing the term 'disease concept' (meaning that alcoholism or drug addiction as a disease is just an 'idea' or theory) for the abbreviated and forthright 'CD disease'. If the reader is convinced that alcoholism and addiction to other drugs are entitled to designation of disease rather than it being a symptom of something else or just a bad habit, then we are probably reading from the same page. In such case you may have little problem in following the reasoning for the treatment approaches discussed later.

Substance dependence has extended its boundaries manyfold since Bill W. and Dr. Bob condensed what they and others before them had learned about alcoholism. From the Alcoholics Anonymous 12-step formula of commitment and changed attitudes and behavior, CD treatment has become an almost limitless hodgepodge of offerings and theories from the professions of medicine, psychiatry, psychology, social work, sociology. hypnotherapy, criminology, religion, psychotherapies, brief therapies, nutrition, physiology, yoga, and even philosophy. The interested person researching the nature of the CD disease probably could arrive to the conclusion that it is whatever one wants it to be. Or even find support for denying that it is even a real disease. To the man with a hammer everything looks like a nail.

The complication of discovering the true nature of the CD disease can be understood when we find that the early research and study of the disease was carried out by persons representing many professional disciplines. Most of these early researchers found their available subjects to be persons (usually men) already diagnosed and in treatment for alcoholism. They found multitudes of sociological and psychological commonalities among these subjects. Those early researchers incorrectly concluded that these frequently found characteristics were pre-existing and were therefore causal factors of the addiction. There was no difficulty in labeling personality traits, psychological problems, and social conditions that seemed responsible for people becoming alcoholic or drug addicted. Those conclusions have proved to be premature. The conditions did prove to be symptoms or the effects of the disease rather than symptoms of other conditions. There are no known traits or conditions that are reliable predictors of future chemical dependence.

Longitudinal studies of non-alcoholic subjects provide strong evidence that the vulnerability factors predictable to future alcoholism or addiction were none of the earlier identified conditions. Familial, twin, half-sibling, and other studies support the evidence that heritability is currently the only reliable factor in identifying those who may be susceptible to addiction. Ongoing longitudinal studies confirm that no psychological, sociological, mental, personality or physical condition has reliable predictability. Conditions that encourage use of psychoactive substances may be considered as risk factors to a susceptible individual.

Brainwave and biochemical/neurological research seems promising in the future identification of what is passed along in families to explain the heritability factor(s). The conditions that create the susceptibility may be one or more biochemical or metabolic anomalies. No one of record has set out deliberately to become alcoholic or addicted. It can be said reliably that most if not all who do develop the disease are initially confident that they can avoid becoming so. No one is able to choose how their metabolic system will function. No one can control or predict prior to usage how their brain chemistry will react to anything they may choose to ingest. No two people metabolize ingested substances in the same way. There is no standard metabolism. The alcoholic or the addict of other drugs cannot learn to use such substances safely. They are unable to change the way their body processes the substances that enter their body. There is no cure for the vulnerability to the CD disease. Not unlike the diabetic, the addict must manage his illness by the practice of abstaining from the substance that is damaging every area of his life and that will eventually destroy him.

The susceptibility to addiction to alcohol seems to exist in about 10% to 15% of American alcohol users. The susceptibility to addiction to other drugs of abuse may be quite different. Crack cocaine, heroin and crystal methamphetamine, for example, are likely to be rapidly addictive to virtually 100% of users. The odds of any person using these highly addictive "hard" drugs without becoming hooked are very poor. By the same token any successful treatment of these drugs is required to be very intense and long term. All addicts are at great likelihood of relapse to active addictive usage.

For all the reasons that we know, the core, the essence, of any successful treatment of chemical dependence must be the achievement of abstinence and the development of defenses adequate to maintaining that abstinence for life. There is no 'cure' of the CD disease, of course. Recovery is the process of halting the progression of the disease and the slow return to the person's pre-addiction state of health. Recovery is the management of one's life despite the chronic condition.

Recovery, as stated above, is grossly oversimplified for the purpose of emphasizing that CD is a disease of itself. Quitting the use of the substance alone will not achieve the state of recovery. Therapeutic abstinence involves numerous steps that return to the CD person control of his ability to choose to remain abstinent and to adapt to an abstinent life style. When that process has been achieved, many if not all, the consequential psychological, sociological, physical and spiritual problems of the disease will return to normal. After extended abstinence and lifestyle changes, if the physical, mental, emotional, or spiritual damage of the disease have not returned to normal, the individual may require specialized treatment.

Chapter II

TREATING CHEMICAL DEPENDENCE

The common denominator in the alcoholic/drug addict population is the exaggerated and/or aberrant effects of usage of a psychoactive chemical. The nature of these effects upon the individual may be as varied as the individuals themselves. The uninitiated are often inclined to paint all addicted persons with the same brush. Victims of the disease are no less likely to stereotype addicts, themselves included, with a variety of prejudicial descriptors, most of which are inaccurate at best and terribly wrong at worst, e.g., all alcoholics are skid-row bums or they are weak and lack willpower. Such stereotypes reinforce the addict's denial process by a resistance to being thus identified, and by providing a faulty example to use as a comparison to their own condition or experience. Each individual addict has had thought processes, mood, personality, inter- and intrapersonal relationships, psychomotor activity, drugging effect, tolerance, behavior, and craving affected by chemical use in unique patterns. Comparing these effects as a means of self-diagnosis can lead to the rationalization that "I'm not like that", or "I have never done that", therefore, "I'm not alcoholic or addicted." It follows that when the chemically dependent person is fully aware of his own unique reactions to chemicals and their own point of progression in the continuing pattern of deterioration, reality comes clearer, the problem becomes personalized, and the denial of it less likely. The client usually requires repeated review of the accumulated effects of the illness which culminated in the need for treatment. No negative consequence of the illness should be ignored, rationalized or minimized. A full catalog of her own unique signs of the illness, recognized and claimed as her own, will put teeth in the person's view of AA's Step 1, "We admitted we were powerless over alcohol (substituting their own drugs of choice) and our lives had become unmanageable".

Alcoholism is a biochemical dysfunction of sedative metabolism, resulting in exaggerated and/or aberrant effects from alcohol (and some other chemicals). Just as the diabetic is benefitted by knowledge and understanding of his illness, the addicted person can likewise benefit by knowledge and understanding of alcoholism and other addictions. It is undisputed that chemically dependent persons are intelligent people and they should be treated as such. Chemical dependence treatment should not be delivered as are some treatments for mental illness, in a cloud of mystique and an attitude that the client probably can't understand the strategies being used by the superior therapist. The alcoholic and addict need to know the what and why of their treatment, and what is valuable and important in the progressive state of recovery because the long-term nature of recovery puts the recovery in the hands of the client himself for most of the course of the illness. The recovery from a chronic illness is to a large extent a matter of successful life-management. In other words, the addicted person must learn in a profound way what is required of the management of one's life despite having an incurable condition. The other side of this admonition is that attempting to teach the chemically dependent person anything not practical to immediate sobriety or long-term recovery may be contrary to sound treatment goals.

The alcoholic or other drug addict invariably enters treatment suffering from at least some and more often many of the physical, mental, emotional, social, and spiritual damages characteristic of the illness. Traditional lore has it that chemical dependence occurs in the sequence of spiritual deterioration, social deterioration, emotional problems, and finally the deterioration of the mind and body. Recovery stages prove to be more effective when they follow that sequence in reverse order, beginning with attending to the direct and indirect damages to the physical part of the problem, primarily the cessation of alcohol and/or drug use. This also involves the medical and nutritional aspects of the treatment and environmental issues.

Chemically induced psychopathology will clear spontaneously with good medical and nutritional care and abstinence from the offending and other psychoactive drugs. Chronic organic brain syndrome may reveal itself as problems of memory and comprehension. Much of the problems of memory may also clear in time, however in some cases two or more years of abstinence may transpire before there is observable improvement. A goal for such individuals should be to acquire a healthy hope for future memory improvement, but with reasonable expectations as to how long and under what conditions (abstinence) that hope may be realized.

The emotional or psychological damage resulting from the illness provides early clues to diagnosis. Among such treatable damages are denial defense systems and manipulative coping mechanisms, overreaction to stress, sleep disturbances, anxiety, and depression. Clean and sober time is on the side of the client in dealing with these problems. An understanding that many of these emotional problems are consequential to the illness is essential as is the learning or relearning healthy ways of coping and finding peace of mind.

Most immediately needed by the newly recovering person is a range of healthy psychological defenses and social skills. Abstinence alone is not treatment. Recovery in the fullest sense of the word means the whole person getting well: mind, body and spirit. Wellness cannot be achieved in a vacuum, in isolation. The recovering person must learn to live in the world with other people. The distorted interactions with others that were necessary to maintaining the addiction are unusable in recovery because they are inadequate for healthy relationships in the real world. The recovering addict must learn to find and maintain healthy relationships with others even while many of them may see him as a "social deviate", i.e., a non-drinker and non-user living in a drug-oriented society. A drug-free haven, such as AA is necessary but ultimately is not enough. The recovering addict can run but he can't hide - forever. At some early point for most there will be the unavoidable exposure to that part of our society which considers alcoholic beverages as standard fare - a customary fact of life, and which makes use of a huge range of readily available chemicals to cope with life's pains and problems. The recovering person must learn the skills and the urgent necessity of remaining clean and dry in the face of all this.

In large part, the strength to accomplish the task of living in the world comes from within. In the secret caverns of the soul of most if not all active alcoholics and drug addicts is a badly mauled and damned self-image. The full and positive restoration of the self-image may be a long and arduous task. The accomplishment of that task must begin in the very early stages of treatment and recovery. A major change in how the person views himself and to expect a positive acceptance by others in the world begins with the regaining of self-respect. More than any other group in the world, the staff of a chemical dependency treatment program must know the value of self-respect and be capable of giving respect to the persons in their charge. This requires a careful avoidance of degrading confrontations and image destroying relationships. Expectations of client behavior should be no different than that expected of staff. The culture of the treatment milieu should be one of caring and respect for staff and client alike. It should be unmistakably business-like in its primary purpose of getting people well from chemicals. Schedules and policies should be clearly communicated to and understood by both clients and staff. It should be clear to the client that she must adhere to the same standards as the staff, i.e., there is no double standard of respect or dedication to purpose for client and staff. Self-image work on an individual basis in group or individual counseling will be reinforced by staff behavior and the atmosphere of the facility environment.

Personal responsibility is the antithesis of enabling behavior. Personal responsibility is the foundation for the reentry into the real world of sobriety. The adoption of an internal locus of control by the addicted client represents a one hundred and eighty degree change of direction. To make this drastic change, the client must experience life without enablers. The client must accept the responsibility for doing everything for himself that he is capable of doing. Conversely, the staff must not do for the client anything he or she is able to do for herself. Rescuers are patently unhealthy for the recovering client. Taking responsibility for someone is first a convenience for the recipient, then an expectation, and finally perceived as a necessity. It becomes a regressive process whereby the rescued, the person being treated as helpless, incompetent and pitiful, comes to believe he is helpless, incompetent and pitiful, and a victim who is increasingly in need of someone or something to take care of him. The addict has first learned to turn to the bottle, the fix or the pill to take care of his needs or to avoid her responsibilities. He or she quickly learns he must have human rescuers who will nurse him when he is sick, bail him out of jail and financial jams, be his patsy and his connection, pick up his socks, and be his shield from the heat of a demanding world. The breaking through deeply entrenched patterns of dependency on a network of human rescuers may be more difficult and equally as important as breaking the grip of the addicting drug. Of course it is not as though the alcoholic/addict is incompetent to care for himself. The CD person has already proven daily his competency by overcoming whatever odds necessary to secure the drug of choice and to find and recruit a network of rescuers to enable him to continue the relentless pursuit of chemical relief called intoxication.

What are the realistic goals for the chemically dependent person? First and last is abstinence and whatever is needed to make abstinence a reality. Nothing more. Nothing less. So simple yet so complex an order. For the counselor/therapist the challenge is great, for we are engaged in the activity of treating unique individuals suffering from greatly varying stages of humankind's most insidious disease. We are challenged to take in persons bankrupt in some or even all areas of their lives, persons whose lives are out of control, having become incapable of making rational decisions, transformed by the effects of a chemical into a caricature of their former real selves, and to give them the enlightenment and the tools by which they can manage their lives independently of chemicals or dysfunctional relationships. He can regain responsibility for every aspect of his life, including his own recovery, only excepting an inability to change how his body metabolizes addictive substances.

Chapter III

ASSESSMENT AND DIAGNOSIS

Alcohol and other drug addiction is defined by the characteristic behaviors of preoccupation with the acquisition of alcohol or other drugs, their compulsive use despite adverse consequences, and a pattern of relapse to alcohol or other drug use despite efforts to quit. All these behaviors reflect loss of control (Miller, 1995).

The condition of loss of control of use of a substance includes loss of quantitative control, i.e., loss of control of how much will be used; loss of control of time or place, i.e., compulsive use; and loss of control of behavior subsequent to use, i.e., failure to limit behaviors when using within social, health, or legally accepted parameters. Any and all these control problems imply that the individual's control of himself has become vested in the demands of the disease state.

There are a number of compelling reasons that an accurate assessment and diagnosis of chemical dependence are necessary:

1. To confirm the existence of the chemical dependence disease: An accurate diagnosis is necessary to assure that the treatment is directed toward the addictive disease rather than some other.

2. To determine the appropriate level of treatment required: Life-threatening conditions may result from certain chemical use or the withdrawal from them, or a self-destructive potential may exist due to psychological consequences of the disease. A clear history is necessary to gauge the level of accumulated deterioration and damage to health, social structures, environment, and personality. Previous history is very significant in this regard.

3. To gather diagnostic data necessary to justify treatment admission, treatment approval by third-party payers, and the need for special assessment processes such as any potential coexisting psychiatric disorder.

4. To answer client and family questions about the reliability of the diagnosis.

5. To gather a concrete history of consequences of the compulsive substance use, preoccupation, progression, relapses, and related behaviors for specific future clinical use to challenge treatment resistance.

A number of different approaches to assessment and in perceiving the disease will be offered. A number of them will be examined. A so-called Public Health Disease Model follows. It will be noted that the Susceptibility and other factors are determined by signs, symptoms and diagnostic history.

The Public Health Disease Model
The Three-Legged Stool

A. A Susceptible Host:
   (Often undetected or undetectable
      prior to onset of the disease).
   Pre-illness susceptibility indicators:
   CD family history
   High 'natural' tolerance
   Experiences high level of subjective
      positive effects from substance use
   Substance used as self-medication
   Heavy or frequent 'recreational' use
   External locus of control
   Experimentation with illicit drugs.
PLUS+
B. An Addictive Substance:
   Alcohol
   Psychotropic medications (prescribed and OTC)
   Illegal drugs
   Addictive non-food or non-beverage substances
      e.g., volatile hydrocarbons, Pam, whiteout, etc.
PLUS+
C. A Compatible Environment:
   Easy availability of addictive substances
   Alcohol or drug using associates
   Social setting accepting of substance use
   Social setting tolerant of substance abuse
   Leisure activities involving substance use.

**EQUALS = THE DISEASE OF CHEMICAL
DEPENDENCE/ADDICTION.**

Absence of any one of the three 'legs' would have prevented the disease from occurring. After the disease exists, treatment strategy would call for the removal of one of the 'legs'. Since doing away with the susceptible host is out of the question, and ridding him of his susceptibility factor is not possible, treatment is limited to removing the addictive substance and/or creating an environment that is not compatible to the existence of the disease. The changeable elements, other than a lifetime of institutionalization, are in the hands of the addicted person. It is only the victim who, in the long run, has the ability to prevent addictive substances from encountering his susceptible person. He also has the ability to change some of his environment and his relationships to make them compatible to abstinence. Expand this formula to include the strategies to accomplish the desired changes and to begin the repair of the disease's damages, and we have a synopsis of effective CD treatment.

Signs of Drug Addiction/Dependence
(Established by interviews of client and others and by observation.)

• Loss of or decrease in the ability to choose when, where, and how much to drink or use, thus affecting rational decision making, exercise of duties and responsibilities, adherence to social mores or customs, maintaining healthy relationships, or preserving good health practices.

• Continued use despite contraindications, e.g., harm to relationships, harm to economic state, harm to social position, harm to physical or mental health, or harm to educational or life goals.

• Life problems resulting from alcohol or other drug use.

• Denial of cause and effect relationship bet
and life problems, e.g., DUIs, job losses, famil

• An irrational willingness to risk legal difficui
career or career goals, relationships, reputation , ~y use
of illegal drugs or illegal use of legal drugs (i.e., breaking the
law for the drug effect).

• A subjective "need" of a drug to cope with problems, to
feel self-confident, or to feel normal.

• Attitudes or repeated behaviors inconsistent with values
held pre-alcohol/drug use.

• Drug/alcohol use seen as problematic by family, friends,
employer, or self.

• The need for a conscious and deliberate effort to 'control'
the use of alcohol or other drugs. (non-addicted persons
don't find it necessary to struggle to refrain from the use of
illegal drugs or over-use alcohol).

• The failure at attempts to quit use or to 'control' use of
alcohol or other drugs.

The forgoing 'symptoms' are effect-based results of
alcohol and or other drug use in excess of use that produces
no problems or harm in any area of a person's life. The existence of only one of the conditions listed provides a strong in-
dication of chemical abuse, incipient chemical dependence,
or a serious lack of good judgment or insight. Two or more of
the listed conditions indicate a state of chemical dependence
- a highly destructive state.

A means of validating the use of effects-based
conditions in the assessment for chemical dependence is to
reverse the nine CD types of drug/alcohol use effects, referred to as 'symptoms', into nine statements of the absence

CD effects. The absence of all adverse drug-use effects in responding to the nine reversed statements indicates the absence of CD. The following are examples of the reversed statements.

1. The ability to freely choose when, where, and how much to use or drink as demonstrated by never having duties, responsibilities, social behavior, relationships, or health harmed by use of alcohol or other drugs.

2. Has never used alcohol or drugs when to do so would have knowingly caused or exacerbated health or other problems.

3. There are no existing life problems resulting from alcohol or drug use. Has a realistic view of how abuse can affect one's life adversely.

4. Refuses to risk legal problems, career, relationships, reputation, etc., by the use or possession of illegal substances, or by the excessive use of alcohol or other legal drugs.

5. Experiences no subjective 'need' to use chemical substances to build self-confidence or to feel normal.

6. Has never compromised accepted values to justify the use of drugs.

7. Family, friends, employer, and self all believe that he has no problems due to drug/alcohol use.

8. The need to 'control' the use of alcohol or drugs is not an issue, and does not require a conscious or deliberate effort.

9. Has neither failed at nor found it necessary to attempt quitting the use of drugs/alcohol.

A truthful positive response to all of these nine statements would be impossible for a chemically dependent diagnosis. The CD counselor is not likely to get nine such positive and truthful answers in an assessment interview. A CD individual heavily in denial may attempt to sound so problem-free. Denial of chemical use problems when otherwise obvious is itself a reliable diagnostic indicator

Criteria for Psychoactive Substance Dependence Diagnosis

There are two widely recognized sources of diagnostic criteria for Substance Dependence and Substance Abuse. The first is from the American Psychiatric Association. In its Diagnostic and Statistical Manual of Mental Disorders, Fourth Edition (DSM-IV), seven criteria are declared, with the occurrence of at least three of them in the same 12-month period being required for the diagnosis of Substance Dependence. The substance(s) involved are to be indicated and whether the condition is either with or without physical dependence should be specified.

See the appendix of this book for a working form (questionnaire) that may be used to systematically record the diagnostic criteria identified. Most hospitals and many HMOs require the use of the DSM-IV diagnostic codes. The DSM-IV also offers criteria for Substance Abuse which requires meeting only one of four listed criteria occurring in a 12 month period, and the stipulation that the subject has never met the criteria for Substance Dependence.

Diagnosis of a psychoactive substance disorder would generally involve meeting the criteria of the disorders as defined by the American Psychiatric Association's or other widely accepted standards. Individuals admitted for treat-ment are expected to have met these criteria. Exceptions would be persons requiring further assessment or those who would benefit from a low level of therapeutic involvement. Diagnostic assessment typically can be accomplished in two to four hours with adult clients.

A similar diagnostic system is the International Statistical Classification of Mental and Behavioral Disor-ders (I'D-10), of the World Health Organization, 1992. DSM-IV and I'D-10 have a common numbering system and other similarities. Clinicians and institutions in the United States usually use the DSM-IV. The I'D has six criteria for Substance Dependence, of which three or more must have been experienced or exhibited some time during the previ-ous year. Note that the I'D-10 places more emphasis on the physical medicine aspects (tolerance and physiological with-drawal) than the DSM-IV. The six criteria for the I'D-10 Substance Dependence are listed for the reader's convenient comparison.

Substance Dependence Criteria (I'D 10)
World Health Organization

1. Difficulties in controlling substance taking behavior in terms of its onset, termination, or levels of use.

2. A strong desire or sense of compulsion to take the substance.

3. Progressive neglect of alternative pleasures or interests because of psychoactive substance use, increased time necessary to obtain or take the substance or recover from its effects.

4. Persisting with substance use despite clear evidence of overtly harmful consequences, depressive mood states consequent to heavy use, or drug related impairment of cognitive functioning.

5. Evidence of tolerance, such as that increased doses of the psychoactive substance are required in order to achieve effects originally produced by lower doses.

6. A Physiological withdrawal state when substance use has ceased or been reduced, as evidenced by: the characteristic withdrawal syndrome for the substance; or use of the same (or a closely related) substance with the intention of relieving or avoiding withdrawal symptoms. (Source: National Institute on Drug Abuse. http://www. nida.nih.gov).

ALCOHOLICS ANONYMOUS

A third and very concise criteria is given in Step One of the Alcoholics Anonymous program: "We admitted we were powerless over alcohol – that our lives had become unmanageable."

The counselor who is knowledgeable about alcoholism and other drug dependencies, and who has an in-depth experience of working with chemically dependent people gains an uncanny ability to intuit the presence of the disease at first sight. Certainly, following a 15 to 20 minute interview, an experienced chemical dependency counselor can recognize patterns of thinking, feeling and behaviors that are uniquely characteristic of individuals conditioned to the disease. That is a most beneficial talent that is often used to let the new client know that he can't successfully deny, minimize or otherwise cover up the existence of the disease.

Such use of that intuitive ability has several drawbacks. Instead of forcing the client to be openly honest, it may result in his being closed, more devious, and passive aggressive, if not openly hostile, toward the counselor. The counselor's ego may be fed by the tactic, but he really isn't plowing new ground. The typical alcoholic/addict has almost surely dealt with similar charges from many people before he ever appeared in the counselor's presence. In other words, hearing such a direct confrontation may do little toward eliciting sincere commitments to recovery.

Another undesirable result is for the client to become compliant, emulating the presumed behavior of the model client. Compliance, paradoxically, is not a guaranteed positive change in behavior. It may be a well established pattern of alcoholic/addict behavior in which the person obeys all the rules, follows all the scheduled activities, always gives the responses most pleasing to the counselor, and says or does whatever is necessary *to keep the counselor and others off his back!* Promises, promises! This Compliant Client is a good bet to be the first to return to drinking and using after treatment. We can't say the resumption of drinking or using is a relapse because, in truth, he had never really sincerely deviated from addictive thinking and behavior from the beginning.

THE CHEMICAL DEPENDENCY DISEASE
The public health disease model as applied to addiction:

Susceptible Person(?)	+ Addictive Substance +	Compatible Environment =	Addictive Disease
Dependent Personality (Pre-drug use)	+ Addictive Substance +	Compatible Environment =	Addictive Disease? (Only sometimes)
Compulsive Personality (Pre-drug use)	+ Addictive Substance +	Compatible Environment =	Addictive Disease? (Only sometimes)
Depressed Person (Pre-drug use)	+ Addictive Substance +	Compatible Environment =	Addictive Disease? (Only sometimes)
Asocial Personality Pre-drug use)	+ Addictive Substance +	Compatible Environment =	Addictive Disease? (Only sometimes)
Blue-eyed Person (Pre-drug use)	+ Addictive Substance +	Compatible Environment =	Addictive Disease? (Only sometimes)

-- and --

Introverted Person			
Extroverted Person			
Trauma Victim	Addict. + Subst. +	Compatible Environment =	Addictive Disease? (Only sometimes)
Victims of Neglect or Abandonment			
Persons from Dysfunctional Families etc., etc.			

There is no known <u>commonly identified</u> psychological trait of alcoholics which pre-dated their alcohol use.

Chapter IV

COLLECTING AND USING
ASSESSMENT DATA

How may an assessment serve also as a positive counseling experience? To answer this question, it is proposed that the assessment take the form of a Socratic dialogue whereby the answers to the counselor's questions in effect lead the client to make her own diagnosis. A careful search for the phenomenological signs of the addictive illness must be made. Directing the focus upon the symptoms which can be observed, in other words apparent to the senses and can be described, the phenomena helps to secure them in memory.

As stated earlier, the illness is defined by behaviors related to preoccupation, compulsive use, denying or ignoring adverse consequences, relapses, and incidents of loss of control. The late stage alcoholic and, at times, the veteran drug addict, may be diagnosed by clinical medical evidence, such as organic brain syndrome, cirrhosis of the liver, pancreatitis, peripheral neuropathy, or other physical damage. The counselor's goal should be to intervene and treat the person much earlier in the progression of the disease.

Therefore, it is crucial to be able to construct a conclusive diagnosis based on other than just tolerance and withdrawal symptoms. Even the regular non-addicted user develops some tolerance. Is there a difference, other than degree, between 'hangover' miseries and 'withdrawal symptoms'? The patterns of addictive thinking, feeling and behavior provide the most telling evidence. Furthermore, the patterns of thinking, feeling and behaving are unique among individuals. It is important that each addicted client recognize, acknowledge, and understand his own unique phenomenological pattern of symptoms and experiences that will constitute an effect-based assessment.

Interpretation of the various diagnostic phenomena to be listed here will no doubt differ from counselor to counselor. As a professional counselor, you are asked to bear with the writer in the effort to identify the major observable or experiencable signs of addiction, acknowledging that most of them will be learned about through self-report of the possibly addicted person. You will have already become familiar with most, if not all, of the signs mentioned. The list will not be exhaustive. The writer's implication of the weight or significance of the signs mentioned may not be universally accepted.

Many of the apparent addiction-related behaviors cannot stand alone in support of the addiction diagnosis. We cannot seek diagnostic proof in a search for the disease's cause. We should look for an array of relevant clues that tell us, and particularly the client, that the subject's life is out of control and unmanageable, that his health and or social structure is failing, that his inability to see what is happening to him is a serious impairment, and that much, if not all, of the negative events in his life are directly or indirectly related to his alcohol or other drug dependence. Alcohol or other drug addicted people are not different from the rest of us except for the active disease.

Quantity or frequency-of-use data are of little value in diagnosis. Rather than the counselor risking the client's probable minimization of these statistics, postpone the request for such information until denial of the illness has been resolved.

There is an important exception to the foregoing suggestion. Where there may be a possibility of severe withdrawal from alcohol or another sedative hypnotic, every effort must be made to determine the time and quantity of last usage (Don't count reduced 'tapering-off' drinking here), the amount of daily use during the past two to three weeks, and the person's history of previous withdrawal episodes. Third-party confirmation of this information is valuable. These precautions can allow early medical intervention if necessary to abort or minimize an episode of delirium tremens, suicidal depression, or severe withdrawal trauma, depending on the drug(s) involved. The confirmed data is needed if authorization for hospitalization must be cleared through a managed care organization. See the Appendix for charts showing the possible relationship of daily drinking to the severity of alcohol withdrawal complications, and signs of withdrawal from the major drugs.

Withdrawal from drugs other than sedative hypnotics are considered by many HMOs not to be life threatening and, therefore, not requiring hospitalization. This position is opposed by some, especially as to narcotics. When in doubt, secure an immediate assessment by a physician. Some counselors work in settings where they may be called upon to assess persons who have severely overdosed on alcohol or other drugs. These situations may be medical emergencies, and that determination should also be made by a physician.

Not infrequently the CD professional will be approached by someone concerned about their alcohol or drug use, but whose use doesn't adequately fit the chemical dependence criteria. Telling such a person, "You aren't ill enough for treatment," is tantamount also to saying to her, "Come back when you are sicker." This situation may justify a 'substance abuse' diagnosis and a less intense level of treatment.

There may be little difference between the alcohol or drug abuse label and the dependence/addiction label. If problem use or concern about use exists, the CD process has begun. That is, if the person has concerns about his drinking or use, that concern is symptomatic of the illness. The reaching out for help calls for a helping response, i.e., treatment. A pattern or repetition of 'abuse' episodes is surely an early stage of chemical dependence. Care should be taken not to discount or belittle the needs of the person at the 'abuse' level.

Metzger suggests that a decreasing ability to make choices about 'using' marks the progressive nature of alcoholism. We may assume that the abuser retains a greater ability to choose, but the illness process has begun. A person who expresses concern about his alcohol or drug use has the illness. The concerned drug abuser is the drinker who spends his time in bars or other drinking situations. Even when he apparently has not had any drinking related problems, he can be in the early stage of alcoholism. (Jellinek referred to this as the "prodromal stage" of the illness.) If the harmful drinking is symptomatic of an underlying susceptibility, the alcohol abuser has already crossed the so-called invisible line in the process of addiction.

If the assessment of a person indicates her to be in that early stage, educational counseling may be all she may need, since at that early stage she still may have some 90% of her capacity to make choices about drinking and related behavior. The counseling goal would be for the abuser to choose and practice abstinence.

The assessment interview should be in a quiet non-threatening setting with a minimum possibility for interruption. Creating rapport with the person is very important and can be accomplished by reflecting a friendly and caring attitude. Really listening to what the person has to say is an active process and necessary at this time. Don't use a joking or insincere tone in asking questions. Don't use judgmental phrasing to the questions. The person herself and what she has to say are important and should be treated with respect.

Ask probing questions to identify continuing impairment of social, occupational and/or psychological functioning that may have predated the alcohol or drug problem, whether or not it may have a cultural or mental/emotional illness source. Such clues can motivate a decision to treat as a dual diagnosis, call for a more in-depth mental/emotional health assessment, or indicate a need for intensive case management. The key objective is to look for the coexistence of drugs and trouble.

Prior to and during the assessment interview, observe for breath odor, tremors, jaundice of skin or eyes, signs of injury, falls, accidents, violence (scars, bandages, limping, signs of soreness, swelling or bruises). Record observations and the person's explanations. Again, don't accuse, confront, or sharply question.

"What prompted you to seek treatment (help) today?"

"When was the last treatment (counseling) you have had for alcohol or drug use?"

"What happened to make that necessary?"

"Was that outpatient or inpatient (residential)?"

"Have you tried to quit on your own?"

"What happened?"

There is the tendency for the alcohol or drug dependent person to relapse after attempts to abstain either in or out of treatment. Be mildly persistent for an answer to the following inquiry:

"What did you do or not do that defeated your effort to quit drinking (or using)?"

"What does your family think about your getting help for your alcohol or drug problem?"

"Tell me about your family situation." (Identify divorces, separations, child custody problems, other family conflicts, drug abuse or alcoholism by others in the family, client's role in the family).

"How did you find out about this treatment program?"

"Where are you employed?"

"Does your employer know you are getting help?"

Social, family and job pressures indicate an existence of problematic use despite the person's denial of it.

"Who referred you for treatment?"

"Why were you referred here?"

"Do you have any outstanding legal problems?"

Referral from a social service agency, the criminal justice system, or a medical professional is strong evidence that addictive behavior has resulted in problems in one or more of these areas. Coercion by an employer to get treatment may be a stronger incentive to follow through if the person has a strong work ethic or relies on the financial resource of the job to support the addiction.

A 'test' series of questions : "How many cups of coffee do you drink daily?" Later, "How many cigarettes do you smoke daily?" (Observe the level of specificity in these two answers). Then ask, "How many drinks (rocks, blunts, etc.) per day?" Is the interviewee more vague about this answer? If so, the change in answering style may indicate denying or minimizing of alcohol or drug use behavior.

"Have you ever had counseling for a mental or emotional problem?"

"Have you ever been depressed? What did you do about it?"

"Have you ever experienced blackouts? Tell me about them."

If the person doesn't know what a blackout is, explain that it is a kind of amnesia. Observations should have tipped off the interviewer whether the person being interviewed is intoxicated or stoned. Postpone asking about this until questioning about using patterns have been completed.

"How often do you drink or use per week?"

"How much do you drink/use each day?"

"Where do you drink/use?" (Not addresses).

"Who do you drink/use with?" (Don't ask for names).

"What else are you doing when you drink/use?" (gamble, talk, watch TV, eat, have sex, etc.)

You should also learn the person's route(s) of ingesting the drug(s) he uses. (IV, inhalation, snorting, drinking, etc.).

"Are you familiar with Alcoholics Anonymous or Narcotics Anonymous?"

"Have you ever been to an AA or NA meeting?"

"What do you know about AA and NA?"

"Have you ever heard that alcoholism (drug addiction) is a disease?"

"What do you think about that?"

"Tell me again, what happened that caused you to come in for counseling today?"

"Do you believe that you may have an alcohol or drug problem?"

"Do you think you need treatment?"

For a yes answer:

"What do you want to get from treatment?"

For a no answer:

"How can we be of help to you?"

By this point the interviewee has either: been relating openly about having a problem; denied, evaded, or given contradictory answers to the questions. The counselor has not expressed an opinion, confronted, or otherwise voiced her assessment. If the counselor has detected from the information given that the interviewee is either abusing or dependent on alcohol or other drugs, she should now tell the interviewee in a neutral manner his diagnostic indicators of substance dependence. Among those possibly revealed in the interview are:

Felt the need to stop drinking or using.

Failed in attempts to stop drinking or using.

Relapsing after a period of abstinence.

Family or relationship problems due to chemical use.

Legal problems related to chemical use.

Health problems caused or worsened by chemical use.

Episodes of drinking or using more than intended.

Drinking or using at inappropriate times or places.

Used alcohol or drugs when doing so put the person at risk of physical harm, loss of job, arrest, conflict with family, or resulted in failure to fulfill family, job, education, or social obligations.

Experiences shame, guilt or remorse as the result of alcohol or drug influenced behavior.

Denies chemical dependence problem despite clear evidence of drug or alcohol related difficulties.

"After reviewing the alcohol or drug related problems you have shared, do you believe that you are alcoholic or drug dependent?"

"Who is pressuring you to get help?"

If the response is a negative despite the evidence of his own answers to previous questions, review his answers or contradictory statements, explaining the connection between his answers and the diagnostic indicators. At each point of correlation between his answers and the indicators, seek his recognition and agreement. Then ask again, "Do you think you are alcoholic or drug dependent?" An affirmative agreement will allow documenting the person's acceptance of the diagnosis. Future denial or doubts about his illness can be responded to from the record of the interview.

The interview may now be completed by eliciting any necessary details of the diagnostic indicators he has supplied. Answers regarding frequency and quantity of use are apt to be more factual now that the emotional hurdle of admission to the problem's existence has been overcome.

The understanding of the disease of chemical dependence requires more than the snake-oil salesman's, "Just trust me."

Substance abuse education, to be effective, must be aimed at the client's intellect. Being chemically dependent is not a sign of mental deficiency. There is now available a great body of scientific evidence and an even greater body of experience that give credibility to classifying alcoholism and drug dependence as a disease. But even intelligent people can have strong beliefs that are founded only on hearsay or unsubstantiated misinformation. When this is the case, it may be necessary to present the evidence as clearly and completely as possible and then challenge the doubtful client to keep an open mind and give the treatment regimen an honest chance to work.

Hopefully, you can be positive about your own convictions that substance dependence is a biopsychosocial-spiritual illness. It is an illness that encompasses all four of these elements. All four of them need to be addressed in logical sequence in the process of its treatment - after first being sure that the client has recognized that he has an illness for which he needs help in overcoming.

Some food for thought: When anti-disease theorists say to the alcoholic/addict, "You aren't really ill from a disease," are they not implying that no treatment is necessary or possible? How does one treat a non-illness?

Readiness for Treatment

A clear diagnosis of chemical dependence and the level of treatment need is the first step in determining treatment readiness. The prospective chemically dependent client's signs and symptoms must indicate the existence of CD and not some other disorder. The assessment must identify any existing signs and symptoms that may indicate the coexistence of an emotional or mental disorder that is not a consequence of the CD itself. It is extremely difficult, and at times impossible, to make an accurate first assessment dual diagnosis decision with advanced cases of chemical dependence.

Determination of the perceived necessity to enter treatment, whether willingly or under coercion, is the next step in arriving at a decision on treatment readiness. These issues may be considered under the heading of motivation. Most counselors are aware that there is no infallible way of predicting a prospective CD client's future behavior. Therefore such judgments are at best based on the most reliable information that can be had at the time of the assessment, placing such a judgment subject to future reconsideration.

An aid to making a treatment readiness decision is a careful coverage of the conditions needed to follow the treatment process. Such conditions include the person's available time to attend the scheduled treatment sessions, the times (and willingness) to attend 12-step meetings, transportation resources, job and other obligations, child care, legal restraints, and others. See an example of an "Eligibility Questionnaire" in the Appendix.

The determination of the level of treatment need, both intensity and type, and the person's ability to meet the conditions necessary for delivery of the services to him, is the third step of readiness determination. The last step is discovering the availability of the level and type of treatment indicated. The obvious must be mentioned here. The task of balancing the client's perceived treatment needs, the availability of a level of treatment indicated, and an HMO's authorization for treatment can be frustrating. The solution frequently required may be called a best-fit one. An empty bed or a low census should not be the determining factor at the expense of the CD's treatment need.

The appropriateness of choosing specific levels of care to meet individual treatment needs can be based upon some assumptions: 1) Treatment in excess of needs is not helpful, is wasteful of resources, and is economically extravagant. 2) Repeating treatment at the same or lower levels of intensity delivered previously and proven to have failed offers little expectation for current success. 3) Chemical dependence, as do other illnesses, responds best to treatment when the level of need is matched by the same level of treatment resources. 4) Where level of need is unclear, a higher, rather than a lower, level of treatment is called for.

Judging the motivation level of prospective clients is the most subjective of treatment readiness indicators. Refusing a person treatment on the assumed lack of motivation is potentially a serious misjudgment. Most if not all persons anticipating entering a treatment program will display ambivalence over the decision. Such ambivalence may be misinterpreted as insincerity. Neither voluntary nor coerced applicants for treatment are likely to be totally convinced they are really addicted and are hoping for clues that they are not.

Unless a person has been exposed to CD treatment previously, he wants to be shown that your treatment is what he needs, and that your treatment works. The reluctance and unwillingness initially shown will likely be resolved as the early period of treatment progresses.

The CD person's resolve may be strengthened by focusing a part of the initial interview on the harmful consequences he has experienced as a result of addiction-related behaviors or events, and on the progressive disruption of various areas of his life: social, economic, values, relationships, reliability, trustworthiness, etc. Questions directed to these costs of addiction can firm up a shaky belief about just how serious his illness is. In the same vein, being convinced of the seriousness of his illness can evoke a greater willingness to make sacrifices to get the treatment he begins to see as critical. Motives for seeking recovery can be difficult to evaluate. Following are two example situations.

JACOB AND MONICA

Jacob was a self-professed alcoholic who presented for treatment after his wife had left him and taken with her their two young children. He verbalized that his motivating pain was the disintegration of his family and a resulting severe depression. Jacob freely and frequently stated a desire to overcome his addiction as a means of getting back his wife and children. He was an ideal client - a complier - doing all the 'right' things, deeply involved and dedicated to following his treatment plan - in every way except modifying his treatment purpose - to get well for himself. Jacob stayed clean and dry for six months, gradually drifting away from AA and aftercare and relapsing when it became obvious that his family was not coming back to him.

Monica was a forty year old crack addicted prostitute who had managed to avoid losing her three children to state custody despite her drug problem and her occupation. She was admitted into an intensive outpatient program convincingly motivated to beat her twenty-four year drug history for the sake of her children. Random drug screens proved her failure to achieve abstinence and she continued to 'work the streets' which finally resulted in the *loss of the custody of her children to child protective services. The children taken away, Monica dropped out of treatment. Never underestimate the power of addiction.*

Two factors must be considered in making treatment placement decisions which override the client-treatment match arrived at by other criteria. These factors are: prior treatment failures and availability of the criteria-selected level of care.

Dimensional Admission Criteria

1. Acute alcohol and/or other drug intoxication and/or withdrawal potential;

2. Physical complications;

3. Psychiatric complications;

4. Life-areas impairments;

5. Treatment acceptance/resistance;

6. Loss of control/relapse crisis;

7. Recovery environment.

Adapted from: *The Cleveland Admission, Discharge & Transfer Criteria: Model for Chemical Dependency Treatment Programs.* Greater Cleveland Hospital Association, Cleveland, OH, 1987.

Assessment Criteria Used for Improper Referrals

1. Person needing inpatient medical care sent to a to non-medical facility.

2. Person needing inpatient psychiatric care referred to outpatient facility.

3. Person with alcohol or drug problem sent to psychiatric unit.

4. Person in need of the controlled environment of a residential alcohol and drug treatment center referred to an outpatient facility.

5. Person with alcohol or drug problem denied admission with no further referral being made.

6. Person not needing acute medical attention referred to a general medical hospital.

The entire assessment interview process must be conducted with compassion and understanding. Even so, readiness for treatment may not be resolved in the initial contact. Ambivalence and uncertainty will often follow the CD person during his full early treatment involvement. The success of Stage I treatment depends upon the genuine acceptance of the client as a person, as an equal who is cared about by the staff. Stage I of treatment is conceptualized in this book as a continuing focus on recognition of the presence and seriousness of the illness, the understanding of why following the steps of recovery is necessary, and to find a level of comfort in being clean and sober.

Chemical Dependency Risk Factors

Risk factors applicable to identifying the existence of CD or that create the potential for succumbing to CD may be described or grouped in numerous ways. One such categorization of factors includes: inherent susceptibility (familial or genetic, biochemical, metabolic, and racial or ethnic);

sociocultural influence (customs and norms of a society or peer group regarding alcohol or other drug use); behavioral/psychological factors (personality traits, mental illness, psychological trauma, development deficiencies, and behavioral conditioning); spiritual and values orientation (external locus of control, ethical standards, life goals, religious guidelines, and self worth).

The pattern and direction of daily choices may inadvertently create susceptibilities to CD, among them: the choices of 'recreational' drugs to use, frequency and quantity of use, set and setting of use, and misinformation about the potential of drug dependency or the means of safeguarding against it.

The categories of risk as offered here are condensed but do incorporate the major risks to the CD disease. Eventually, each recovering chemically dependent person should learn what risk factors apply to him, and they must become part of his relapse-proofing. Whether or not the risks are major ones or not at all, or whether or not they are causes or merely susceptibilities, should not be a disruptive controversy.

Searching for a precipitating cause may only be a rationalization that serves to postpone action when time is of the essence. Predictive medicine or counseling or preventive medicine or counseling must rely on risk-related factors and/or sub-clinical elements. Let it suffice here to say that the solid diagnosis of chemical dependence can, and perhaps should, be made without a detailed analysis of preexisting susceptibilities. However, the conscientious examination of risk factors can make possible an earlier diagnosis, provide confirming data for the diagnosis, be a helpful tool in revealing a client's denial, and provide guides to planning treatment strategy.

Chemical Dependence Resistance Factors

Just as there are susceptibility factors that may predispose an individual to possible chemical dependence, there are also factors of resistance that may provide built-in safeguards against CD. Some of these resistance factors are: adverse physiological reactions to the drug effect; no family history of alcoholism or drug abuse; absence of mental illness; no family history of mental illness; a satisfying time structure (job, hobby, social life and recreation) that doesn't rely on alcohol or drug use; a functional knowledge of addiction/dependence; a wide range of skills for coping with stress; a positive and unconditional self-acceptance; high self-esteem and self-confidence; a strong external support system; an internal locus of control; a capacity for intimacy; risks appropriately in interpersonal relationships; a capacity for insight and self-awareness; not overly exposed to substance abuse by others; and chemical substances not easily accessible.

An absence of any one or a number of these factors does not constitute a cause of CD or mean that the person is at high risk to becoming chemically dependent. Any one of them may serve to defend the individual against the widespread CD disease. The wise rule-of-thumb is that no one is exempt from being susceptible except by total abstinence.

Most, if not all, chemically dependent persons possess a number of characteristics and assets that have been suggested here as CD resistance factors. If an individual has the brain chemistry and or the metabolic make up to react to psychoactive substances to enhance the 'pleasure principle' or to produce a 'need' to repeat the drug/alcohol use experience, and he drinks alcohol or uses drugs, he will likely become CD despite other CD resistance factors. Many of the suggested resistance factors are also positive assets that can be valuable tools in regaining a state of sobriety should chemical dependence occur.

Getting a Complete Assessment

Critical data collected in the CD assessment must be recorded for inclusion in the client's treatment record. This may be done in a free style narrative of the interview or in a formal way as dictated by administrative requirements or the interviewer's recording skills. Acquiring the needed information will depend upon how successfully the interviewer can establish rapport with the interviewee, elicit honest and open responses to the questions, and get all and only that information pertinent to making a diagnosis and an appropriate disposition of the person's intake request.

Some questions and questioning strategies have been suggested, but other information will probably be needed. Following is a list of subjects frequently wanting response to by HMOs, third party payors, treatment planners, the primary counselor, patient records, ancillary treatment resources, and others:

Is this a crisis intake? (medical or psychiatric emergency).

How was a crisis intake responded to?

The source of the referral.

Detail of presenting withdrawal signs and symptoms.

Alcohol and drug treatment history.

Date of last problem use.

Alcohol or drug withdrawal history.

Alcohol or drugs currently in system (last use).

History of withdrawal related seizures, hallucinations, dementia.

Assessment of imminent withdrawal potential.

Suicide or homicide potential, self report.

Suicide or homicide potential as perceived by interviewer.

Action taken in response to suicide/homicide potential.

Current health problems other than CD.

Current medications and prescribing physician.

Mental/emotional status/stability (mental health impression).

Current and pending legal problems.

Relapse history and potential.

Reported relapse triggers.

Perceived strengths relevant to recovery.

Individual's recovery environment.

Assessment of person's ability to cope with problems and stressors.

DSM IV: Axis I (code)_____

DSM IV: Axis II (code)_____

DSM IV: Axis III (self-report of medical conditions)

DSM IV: Axis IV (List psychosocial and environmental problems)

DSM IV: Axis V (Global Assessment of Functioning clinician's judgement)

Recommended treatment level (ASAM criteria)_____

Interviewer's signature and credentials_____

Chapter V

PROGRESSION IN THE CD DISEASE

Alcoholism typically arises at the diagnosable level preceded by a lengthy period of alcohol use and alcohol abuse. There are subtle earlier signs of the progressive illness that usually escape detection by both the victim and most of those around him. Early alcoholism signs are little different from those experienced by "alcohol abusers" or "problem drinkers." The level of individual susceptibility, environmental factors, and other variables are involved in the rapidity of onset of alcoholism ranging for some from the first major use (as recalled by some "instant alcoholics") to after twenty or more years of use.

Alcoholics and non-alcoholics are all different. Every person is an individual. There are also individual variations in the evolution of alcoholism. Variations occur in the rapidity of onset, the progression of symptoms, and the eventual severity of alcoholism (Miller, p. 65). The same statements may also be made about coronary disease and hypertension. When viewing the entire population of alcoholics or other drug addicts, we will see an infinite variety of histories, symptoms, personalities, cultures, levels of severity, and other characteristics. Despite the many identifiable similarities due to the disease, the person must be viewed as a unique individual, related to on the basis of who he is and where he is in his life and in his disease.

The individual uniqueness is a fundamental reason that the "sheep dip" method of treatment will not suffice. The recognition of the progressiveness of the disease and the fact that the illness affects negatively every aspect of the person's being allows for a significant amount of treatment uniformity. Without some uniformity in delivery of treatment, its delivery in a group setting would be ineffective, and individual treatment would require more time in history taking and assessment. Alcoholics and other drug addicts usually present themselves for treatment at a low ebb of their illness, demonstrating a distressing level of symptoms. For this reason most any intervention will produce a significant appearance of early progress. Beyond this, progress involves the coordination and commitment of the CD client.

The patterns of alcoholism progression have changed over the years, probably due to a number of factors. There are few if any "pure" alcoholics anymore. Other drugs, prescription, OTC, or illegal, are almost always involved to accelerate the process. Although a recent study claims to discredit the belief, there is strong case history evidence that the younger a person begins use of alcohol or other psychoactive drugs, the shorter the time of use before addiction may be diagnosed in the susceptible individual. Alcoholism has long been considered selective, occurring only among alcohol users who are vulnerable due to familial predisposition, biochemical susceptibilities, and a variety of other unspecific cultural or environmental factors.

Other "hard" drugs appear to be much less forgiving of heavy or frequent users, with an unknown high percentage of such users becoming dependent within a relatively short time span of use. Regardless of the drug involved or the reasons for using, progression to the disease state can be identified. As discussed elsewhere, discovering the progressive patterns of use, thoughts, feelings, and behaviors are diagnostic keys. They also provide us with a snapshot of the pathways to recovery.

Recovery from addiction also is very seldom, if ever, spontaneous. Recovery is a process, a passage, a series of changes. The progression of recovery has been compared to the teen's journey from childhood to adulthood. Like that of adolescence, the process is painful, confusing, and affected by influences on all sides. The process is a unique experience for each individual. The person is frequently torn between the security of what is and the hope of what could be. From the position of the adolescent or the addict, it is difficult to perceive or to understand an objective rationale for what to do or how to do it.

The fortunate alcoholic/addict is one who finds himself under the guidance of a knowledgeable chemical dependency counselor familiar with the recovery process and its timely stages. The wise counselor is aware that essential steps in the process cannot be passed over, nor can essential steps be forced to occur before their time. The client must be met where he is, given the tools and guidance appropriate to his point of recovery, and be allowed to progress consistent with his readiness to progress.

The notion of the existence of recognizable phases of recovery is not new. Many ways of perceiving the recovery phases have been suggested. A level of validity may be discovered in many of these views. Unfortunately their often homespun, unscientific origins have made them less than widely accepted among traditional health professionals. As a result, many in the treatment field minimize their potency and utility.

Years of experience plus the shared wisdom of many outstanding professionals in the alcohol and drug treatment field have persuaded a firm conviction that treatment of chemical dependence and addiction is a unique process. The effectiveness of this unique process can be founded upon definable recovery phases, and treatment stages, and upon an awareness of addictive behavioral dynamics, addictive cognitive processes, and consequential affective anomalies.

An early formula for understanding both the deteriorative decline into addiction and the phases of recovery from it is the SSEMP-PMESS paradigm. (See Figure 01). The progressiveness of substance dependence is assumed to follow the sequence of deterioration beginning with the individual's spiritual self, followed by the disintegration of social structure and skills, emotional stability, and, unless arrested, mental and finally physical declines. Obviously, these broadly stated sequences do assume a multitude of forms, but the concept does offer major utility. At assessment, for example, an accurate history interfaced with the SSEMP concept can help to pinpoint the person's principle susceptibilities to sabotaging his own treatment, and will help in making an accurate determination of how far the new client's disease has progressed. Armed with an evaluation of the client's liabilities (susceptibilities), and the point of advancement of the disease state, the counselor can make an initial determination of strengths and weaknesses that may affect treatment outcome and help validate a choice of where initial intervention should occur. Generally the PMESS concept suggests that an orderly progression of recovery would expect to be followed in an order inverse to the onset sequence.

Figure 01: The SSEMP-PMESS Paradigm

A broad view of the progression of chemical dependency:

(SSEMP)=SPIRITUAL > SOCIAL > EMOTIONAL > MENTAL > PHYSICAL->

the progressive deterioration of chemical dependence.

(PMESS)=PHYSICAL > MENTAL > EMOTIONAL > SOCIAL > SPIRITUAL->

the progressive phases of recovery from chemical dependence.

Practically, the PMESS concept tells us that attempting to engage the client in restructuring his social life before dealing with critical physical needs (e.g., the need for detoxification, an untreated injury, or a place to live) is a poor strategy. Likewise, attempting to initiate a resolution to spiritual needs while emotional problems still rage may, again, be putting the cart before the horse. Abraham Maslow's hierarchy of need in human growth and development offers an interesting parallel to the PMESS concept. Using the PMESS concept as a tool for teaching some of the dynamics of chemically dependence to a newcomer to recovery or to his family can be effective. Therefore the CD counseling should proceed in the PMESS sequence, beginning with physical needs and changes as the **First Progressive Treatment Principle.**

A close look at the recovery side of the ever present Jellinek's chart reveals another view of the concept of progression in CD recovery. The thirty-odd items on this list can easily involve the work of years. The implication of the behavioral, cognitive and emotional changes toward recovery is that certain ones must occur to prepare a readiness for the next progressive recovery change to be likely. Jellinek is given credit for being perhaps the first to perceive from scientific observation that a process must occur to overcome the disease. Cultural, educational and environmental differences among individuals require some rewording of Jellinek's descriptive words of recovery steps, however, the progressive principle remains relevant today.

Progressive Treatment Principle 2: Expectations of CD counseling and of recovery should reflect logical progressive steps.

The twelve steps of the AA program also are definitely progressive, implying that adopting them and "working" them proceeds logically and sequentially from step-one through step-twelve. The person in need of breaking the grip of the addiction already knows at some level about her powerlessness over the drug and state of unmanageability of her life. Breaking through the denial of powerlessness and life management problems is second only to attending to distracting physical needs among the counselor's priorities. Achieving the client's early abstinence from drug use is another of the counselor's early concerns. If the counselor or the CD person has difficulty with the steps that have a religious connotation, a careful interpretation using the concepts of surrender (Tiebout), acceptance, humility, and the myth of control will bridge the gap. Spirituality is further concerned with qualities of the human spirit such as love and compassion, patience, tolerance, forgiveness, contentment, a sense of responsibility, and a sense of harmony (from the Dalai Lama). Other advantages of the 12-step fellowship program will be discussed later.

Principle 3: Environmental and drug use related changes are of paramount importance in establishing positive recovery progress.

Many authorities in the CD treatment field have observed that the first year of recovery should focus entirely on achieving sobriety. We are also admonished to avoid attempting psychotherapy during the first year of recovery.

Recovering people are noted for their impatience. Counselors and family members, not to mention courts, employers, insurance companies, and others, are also known to be impatient with the seemingly endless counseling and meetings. AA has given recognition of this phenomenon in its slogans "First Things First", "One Day at a Time", and "Easy Does It." A caveat is appropriate here. The focus of the counseling should remain steadfastly on the problems of getting and staying abstinent. Temptations are often strong to digress from the basic early recovery focus and "do therapy". Doing so may actually delay recovery progress. The client will quickly learn that an acceptable diversion from an uncomfortable interaction dealing with the need of a behavioral change is to introduce a "psychological" or "relationship" problem, leaving the crucial issue abandoned.

Principle 4: Early recovery counseling calls for guidance, teaching, support, encouragement, modeling, discipline, direction; not therapy. For the CD client early recovery requires the changes to bring about abstinence and the behavioral/cognitive changes to reinforce that abstinence.

How much time is needed to reach and solidify early recovery goals? Probably at least as long as the individual was a problem or compulsive user of the substance, if she works diligently at making the recovery changes. As Alcoholics Anonymous reminds us, the recovering person is dealing with alcohol (and other addictive drugs) which are cunning, baffling and powerful. There are apparently no reliable short cuts. One way or another, the recovering person will be obliged to touch all the bases on the way home to recovery.

Vernon Johnson, a notable figure in CD treatment, provides us with an expert's opinion of the progressive nature of alcoholism when he defined the disease as primary, progressive, chronic, and fatal.

There is an ongoing debate among AAers from time to time of the accuracy of the term "recovering" versus the possibility of a CD person ever being "recovered". Implicit in this debate is the recognition of the long-term progressive nature of CD recovery. In one bit of recovery lore, old-timer alcoholism counselors have responded to the question, "How long does recovery take?" with the answer, "At least as long as it took for the disease to emerge, no less than 3 to 5 years, plus life-long maintenance." Heeding the mass of input on the credibility of progressive recovery, we may adopt the following Course of Recovery:

1. Recovery must be the primary priority, rather than other issues.

2. Recovery is progressive - not spontaneous, but long term, and will progress in a PMESS sequence.

3. There is no cure - only recovery (the arrest of the destructive progress of the disease).

4. Recovering (recovered?) chemically dependent people can live full and normal lives.

Progression of chemical dependency recovery follows rather predictable phases. Many people have recognized these phases and described them in various ways as we have seen. I have elected to use a 4 phase recovery outline. These phases are not set in concrete and may vary from individual to individual. Using the phases as general treatment parameters can serve to focus the treatment effort appropriately and to maximize its effect in the briefest time possible. A condensed outline of the four recovery phases is offered, followed by a more detailed discussion of the content of Stage I, the most critical stage of treatment.

PHASES OF RECOVERY/TREATMENT

I LIFESTYLE RESTRUCTURING: 1 to 3 months

Abstinence from psychoactive drugs (detox prn, withdrawal from nonessential prescribed medications. Carry out a Quit-Day procedure ASAP and produce negative drug screens)

Environmental changes (establish a drug-free residence, a drug-safe workplace, and drug-free leisure-time places).

Behavioral changes (tell family and friends about your treatment, sever relations with all drug users and dealers, identify and use trigger-free routes to shop, work or play, withdraw from potentially emotion-disruptive relations, say "NO" in words and actions to invitations to drink or use, consciously build and learn to use a personal support system, bond with a 12-step self-help group by frequent attendance and active involvement, get a sponsor, plan specific drug-free recreation and other leisure and social activities).

Cognitive changes (accept having an addictive illness, learn and remember positive benefits of recovery, identify and remember personal signs and symptoms of addiction, learn and understand the disease of addiction, learn and practice HALT and HEDS techniques of neutralizing urges to drink or use, learn and change addictive thinking, learn and identify with the powerlessness and unmanageability language of Step 1 of AA/NA).

Affective changes (bond with treatment group members, ask for support and give support, learn the addict's "landmines" in society's "minefield", learn avoidable and unavoidable triggers and fear them, learn about relapse and its danger signs, emotionally experience the hope of recovery, postpone any major life decisions except to recover from addiction, put staying clean and sober life's first priority). Suggestion: Have client keep a recovery journal to include a careful cataloging of people, places, activities, times, mental states, physical conditions, and thought processes associated with substance use for avoidance or coping.

II SOLIDIFYING RECOVERY: 9 months to 2 years

Continue to strengthen the lifestyle restructuring tasks of Phase I (strengthen bond with non-drug using culture, expand personal support network and practice using it, individualize personal issues at a low intensity [KISS], postpone major relationship changes, postpone psychological issues such as exploring the unconscious or emotional/mental conflicts unless specifically endangering sobriety now. Learn and practice relapse prevention skills, resolve physical and health issues, maintain high level of involvement in treatment activities such as aftercare group and AA, learn and practice good problem solving skills, make constant use of time-structure planning to minimize risk of exposure to unsafe situations. Practice avoidance of triggers, confer with sponsor at least weekly, practice recognition of positive recovery gains by self and others).

III INDIVIDUALIZING RECOVERY: 3 to 5 years

Persevere in following previously learned recovery practices (maintain close ties with drug-free culture and personal support groups, guard abstinence carefully, expand necessary exposure to non-recovering community with caution and be prepared to cease any contacts which may threaten recovery. Reestablish damaged relationships, make amends, repair any career or job damages, get needed psychological and relationship therapy/counseling, focus on spiritual growth, stay close to your sponsor).

IV MAINTAINING RECOVERY: for life

Lifelong abstinence from psychoactive drugs (ongoing attention to healthful living and healthy relationships, maintain contacts with 12-step mutual help group, extended involvement is recommended).

Typical Pattern of Recovery Progression

Developing a Non-Drinking Peer Group Identity

	1st Year	2nd year	3rd Year
Mood Swings	Labile mood Vacillating commit-ment Slips/re-lapses may occur Wavering hope of recovery	Cope with post-acute with-drawal Dependence on AA sponsor Emotional distresses	Growing self-acceptance Post-acute symptoms subside Stress in hand
Task or emphasis	Accepting the illness Getting sober Staying sober Bonding with 12-step group	Setting material world in order	Setting right relation-ships with others

Diagraming the general progress of alcoholism recovery.
Source: Dr. Larry Wharton and others.

Whole Person Recovery Tasks by Recovery Stages

Task areas	Stage I	Stage II	Stage III
Physical	Detox- Drug free Clean up environment Ask for help Bond with self-help group Build support network	Strengthen abstinent lifestyle Attend self-help group frequently Bond with sponsor Attend to physical health	Tend to physical health Stay active
Psyco-logical	Hope of recovery Acceptance of illness	Reward self for recovery gains Improve self-perception Healthy need to make amends	Mental/emotional counseling as needed Resolve relationship issues Do 12-step work
Social	Drug-free leisure activities Drug-free peer group	Learn new drug-free activity Expand drug-free peer group	Expand drug-free support group
Spiritual	Learning I'm OK drug-free Honesty Openness Humility	Acceptance of self & others Feeling rejoined to human race	Experience meaning of Serenity Acceptance of self as OK
Education	Learn about A&D Learn own signs of addiction Learn to cope or avoid triggers	Learn about self Educational self-improvement	Learn about others Stabilize financial & material condition

General Cautions for Recovery Tasks and Expectations:

Year 1: Abstinence

Year 2: Personal (interapsychic) issues & relationship (interpersonal) issues

Year 3: Material reality

Chapter VI

RELATIONSHIP OF CD COUNSELING
TO CD RECOVERY

Any approach to CD counseling must take into account that alcoholism and other drug addiction is a long-term process, viewed in years rather than in weeks or months. As in other chronic diseases, there is no known cure. Recovery consists of a halting of the progression of the illness, a repairing of the damages suffered to body, mind and spirit, and learning to manage one's life with the enduring, chronic susceptibility to relapse, i.e., preventing the return to the active disease state. Most CD counselors seem to agree with this concept and to the idea that at some point the CD person must become fully in charge of, as well as responsible for, his or her long-term recovery state.

The interpretation of this concept has, however, been far from uniform among those who work in the field. At one extreme is the belief that merely achieving abstinence should be an adequate limitation to necessary professional help, with the CD person continuing the recovery process by the application of willpower to stay abstinent.

At the other extreme, conductors of extended programs of four or more weeks in a residential or inpatient setting or in an intensive (long) outpatient program, often advocate a continuance of a professionally run continuing care program for two or more years, augmented by 12-step program involvement even longer. The goal of this approach is to establish such an advanced level of recovery in the client that the person's continuance in self-directed recovery is driven by a deep seated state of conditioning. While practically all CD individuals would fit somewhere within these scopes of treatment, there is certainly no specific time or mode of treatment that will fit all CD victims.

Research results have not been consistent, some concluding that short-term outpatient treatment of CD is as effective as the expensive long-term inpatient variety, others concluding that the longer the person remains in treatment the better the odds that he will remain abstinent and readjusted to a non-addictive lifestyle, i.e., recovering.

Managed care has forced the CD counselors' hands to either fight a surely losing battle for reimbursement by thirdparty payers for long-term treatment, or adopt an approach and methods in a short-term format that is both reimbursable and adequately effective for most clients.

The treatment method recommended in this book is a time-frame concept that seems to comply with the short-term demands of the MCOs. The process is consistent with the recognized progressive recovery/treatment needs. It is diagrammed and outlined as follows in Table 2:

TABLE 2

A	B	C	D	E
prn detox 3 or more days	intensive outpa- tient 4 to 7 weeks	aftercare group self-help group 6 to 12 months	self-help group MH therapy prn 3 to 5 years	life mainte- nance

A. Medically managed inpatient or ambulatory detoxification. The approval for the inpatient level of treatment is rare due to the often absence of life threatening conditions caused by withdrawal from certain classes of drugs, and the now common application of strict and concrete guidelines for hospitalization by third party payers. Hospitalization approval often requires one or more of the following criteria, certified by a physician: withdrawal from a long and heavy episode of alcohol, barbiturate, or narcotics usage; strong suicide potential; or coexisting severe medical problems, all of which could be life threatening or considered to be medical crises.

The average alcoholic or cocaine addict client requires very little in the way of expert medical care and is usually quickly turned over by the physician to the ministrations of CD counselors, AA twelve-steppers, clinical psychologists, or clinical social workers. In fact, according to one poll, the vast majority of physicians regard alcoholism as a treatment entity, but only 27% of those interviewed felt competent to treat alcoholic patients (Niven, 1984); and in a survey of 200 physicians (Goldsmith, et al., 1984), half of them said the medical training they had received about alcoholism had been either "rather" or "completely" ineffective, and most (88 percent) felt they needed more such education and training in how to treat alcoholism patients (Cahalan, 1987).

B. An intensive outpatient program (IOP) of 12 to 20 three-hour sessions (at least three sessions per week) of drug abstinent participation monitored by random urine drug screens (UDSs).

Goals should include heavy emphasis on changes in lifestyle behaviors; assuring a drug-free residence and workplace; severing all associations with drug using or dealing, or alcohol abusing individuals, places, activities, or things; identifying all "triggers" to drinking/using behavior, avoiding those that can be avoided and learning to cope with those that cannot be avoided; building a drug-free personal support network including bonding with a self-help support group by attendance at four or more meetings per week and a solid connection with a sponsor; practicing the writing of a daily detailed plan of safe activities (work, school, treatment and leisure time, and with particular emphasis on weekends and holidays which are especially dangerous for the newly recovering person); and early involvement of the CD's family or a significant other. Relapsing clients should be required to get abstinent and begin the treatment again from the start.

C. Graduates of the program outlined above should be ready for an advanced recovery group meeting weekly for ninety minutes, led by a qualified counselor. The recovering CD should be encouraged to participate in this group for 6 to 12 months. Aims of this group's participants are coping with early recovery issues such as adapting to the straight/

abstinent lifestyle, problem solving, and relationship building. CDs should continue with frequent and deepening involvement with their self-help support group. Persons who are exposed to high-risk home or work situations or continuing difficulty with drug craving are candidates for participation beyond the 6 months minimum.

D. This stage of recovery should find the person ready to begin any needed therapy for unremitted mental or emotional problems. Otherwise, the stage consists of a continuation of the involvement in a 12-step group and any other unfinished goals. This phase of recovery and the preceding one are activated by the individual's motivation and her understanding of its long-term nature. In other words, the active participant knows and understands how to preside over her own recovery and does so.

Early recovery efforts must include assurance that the newly abstinent CD's wish to find instant recovery is futile, and that successful recovery is based on a long-term effort - one day at a time. The recovering alcoholic/addict still working at it in this 3 to 5 year period is often one who has experienced a number of false starts, peppered with relapses, repeated treatments, and recurring problems. Many of us have to learn things the hard way. This stage is a particularly important one for the person working in the chemical dependency field or intending to. A strong recommendation is made that a beginning CD counselor who is recovering have a minimum of three solid years of stable sobriety. The recommendation is based on seeing too many fine potential counselors relapse due to the pressures of this emotionally intense business on a still-fragile recovery base.

The secret of success of a chemical dependency treatment program with abbreviated professional intervention requires a realistic focus on the progressive nature of CD - both of the illness and its recovery. It requires treating the illness as the primary illness that it is and not be diverted into irrelevant therapy byways. The chapter on the Nature of Chemical Dependence is designed to clarify what CD is and what it isn't.

The Therapeutic Content of Stage I Recovery, and the treatment steps to that recovery, follow rather predictable stages. The proposed Chemical Dependence Counseling Method recognizes the four progressive stages previously outlined. The emphasis is upon taking therapeutic advantage of the progressive nature of the CD disease and its progressive recovery. Stage I, labeled Lifestyle Restructuring, may also be called the Cessation of Use Stage. A detailed discussion of focuses and content of this stage follows.

It will be noted that the cessation of use of alcohol and other drugs, and the many strategies to preserve that abstinence, are compressed into a short treatment period. The cessation of substance use and the lifestyle restructuring constitutes an intense, strongly focused stage of recovery. Without the successful incorporation of the Stage I goals and objectives, the probability of the CD person progressing farther in recovery is very slim. The repeated cautions to avoid being sidetracked from the Stage I objectives are reminders of what CD is - a primary disease - not a symptom of psychological or personality problems. Cessation of alcohol and drug use is essential to the arrest of the deteriorating downward slide of the disease. Lifestyle Restructuring is the strategy and the process that can make abstinence a possible reality. The cognitive, affective and behavioral symptoms of chemical dependence were induced by the chemical and the addictive life style. These symptoms will cease or wane with abstinence and the practicing of the recovering life style.

Critical Treatment Tasks for Alcohol and Drug Dependent Clients in Phase I of Recovery

The following list is not entirely in priority order for any particular CD client, except the need to abstain from alcohol and other drugs. Every client may not require concentration on every listed task, and there may be many clients who need to complete tasks not listed. The following tasks are among the many areas of guidance and instruction offered by an intense outpatient program in the process of aiding its clients to build the necessary strengths and skills for recovery.

1. Abstain from use of mood-altering chemicals. Quit drinking and using and produce negative drug screens.

2. Accept having the disease of drug/alcohol dependence. Identify and own their personal signs and symptoms of CD.

3. Learn self-discipline in the compliance with program rules and schedules, and following assigned tasks.

4. Take action to assure a drug-free residence. Have users move out or take steps to move away from an environment hazardous to recovery.

5. Create a drug-safe workplace. Assure that leisure places and times are drug/alcohol-free. Cease association or contact with places and activities where drug and alcohol use occurs.

6. Resolve or cope with legal difficulties. Clean up the past: arrests, child support, debts, etc.

7. Learn to work with others in the treatment group. Give and take supportively with fellow clients.

8. Build a support system both in and out of the program. Complete and adhere to results of Supporters/Neutrals/Detractors form. Contact a supporter to recovery at least once per day.

9. Identify relapse triggers and harmful defense mechanisms. Avoid avoidable triggers. Devise concrete means of coping with unavoidable triggers.

10. Learn how to avoid persons and places associated with alcohol and drug use. Learn and practice skills of advance planning of time-use. Identify and use drug-free escorts when risky areas and places can't be avoided.

11. Become active in AA/NA/CA groups with frequent attendance. Attend minimum of four sessions per week. Secure a same-sex sponsor and talk with him or her weekly.

12. Learn and understand the processes and dynamics of addiction. Become educated in the CD disease.

13. Keep a recovery journal on what has been learned in treatment for future reference. Make entries daily. Discuss in the group.

14. Write a "fire plan" of actions to follow when drug craving occurs. Know specifically what to do to combat the craving and stifle the compulsion.

15. Overcome urges/temptations to leave or shortcut treatment. Interact with staff, fellow clients, sponsor, and supporters when discouraged or impatient.

16. Believe that he/she can get well - if committed to the goal. Can verbalize positive expectations of recovery. Begins accepting self in a positive light.

17. Identify patterns of denial of the illness. Share and explore feelings with others.

18. Write and share a specific action plan for continuing recovery. Work with staff on continuing care plan.

19. Stop blaming others for being in the grips of dependence. Show increased evidence of being responsible for self.

21. Remembers the pain and damage caused by substance use. Avoid recalling alcohol/drug use history as positive.

22. Encourages family or significant other to learn about the disease. Family/significant other attends family sessions.

23. Learn and understand AA Steps 1 and 2. Can express the meaning of these steps and their relationship to his circumstances.

24. Know how to prevent and cope with relapse, one day at a time. Know the early signs of relapse and the defenses against relapse.

25. Learn about and know the defenses against post-acute abstinence syndrome (PAS). Can verbalize the dynamics of PAS and its risks for relapse. Adapt "Fire Plan" as defense against PAS.

26. Be responsible for his own recovery, his own feelings, and his own behavior. Understand the credo, "I am responsible."

27. Accept the nurturing of program staff and fellow clients. Learn the value of nurturing others.

28. Understand the processes of change and why change

is necessary. Can verbalize why being flexible and adaptable are good survival traits. Understand the lessons in the Serenity Prayer.

29. Learn patience, put first things first, put recovery first, function and cope one day at a time.

30. Function in the here-and-now, all we have for sure is today. Avoid worrying about the past or the future.

31. Practice scrupulous honesty in thought, word and deed. Just do it.

32. Have the willingness and wisdom to do whatever is needed to maintain healthy sobriety.

These thirty-two idealized accomplishments bring to mind the AA admonition to seek progress, not perfection. We are all bound by the limitation of doing the best we can. It also seems obvious that dealing with this array of recovery tasks, even when putting them in terms of behavior change and rote learning, is more than enough to occupy the 15 to 40 three-hour sessions estimated for Stage I Lifestyle Restructuring.

Stating the Stage I goals and objectives in the above manner is an oversimplification because some of the tasks require intrapersonal changes. Such changes can occur in the process of completing tasks, when learning eventually produces insight, or they may occur as the result of a specific counseling effort. Most of the tasks in Stage I have emotional aspects as well as cognitive and behavioral ones. Despite Stage I seeming at first glance to be routine and the same for all, in actuality every objective or task, every change, involves thought (clearly understanding why), feelings (grief in losses of the old, fears and uncertainty for the new), and behavior (overcoming the resistance to doing the unaccustomed). Further, each individual is a different person in personality, family custom, environmental conditioning, beliefs, history, culture, and abilities. The CD counselor must make himself aware of these emotional aspects and differences when they emerge, and openly recognize them to the client.

The emotional aspects of Stage I tasks and changes may be addressed by simply acknowledging their existence, or they may call for spending specific time and effort in helping the client understand and cope with them. Seldom is it necessary to devote considerable time in dealing with emotional issues. Some tasks that usually give rise to troublesome emotions are briefly discussed below:

a.   Actually quitting the use of alcohol or other drugs, and any withdrawal that results. This action puts considerable stress on a person's commitment to become abstinent. The action of quitting can strengthen and increase confidence in an individual's self-discipline, while failing to succeed in doing so creates doubts in the ability to overcome the CD illness. Much guidance and support, both emotional and physical, are needed here.

b.   The concept of surrendering as perceived in chemical dependence recovery is often quite different than as seen by the typical man or woman in our society. Surrender can have such negative connotations to a person newly in treatment that the resistance to it is overwhelming. The word's reference to giving up the battle of trying to made the drug work positively, to recognize the existence of the CD disease, the need to be receptive to help from others in overcoming it, and the practice of humility are all critical elements in CD recovery. Careful explanation and assurances of understanding are necessary. The experiencing of the universality of surrender among virtually all recovering chemically dependent persons is most therapeutic.

c.   The feelings of loss and genuine grief are likely to be experienced in the process of accomplishing a number of recovery tasks. Among these are: the cessation of looking to enablers and rescuers to get the CD's needs met; detaching from drug connections and supplier patsies; and separating from the drug using and alcohol drinking social milieus in favor of clean and sober supporters of the CD's recovery. There is very often a genuine emotional bonding with members of these user groups and "abandoning" them gives rise to grief, isolation, and the guilt of seeming to be a traitor. The people in the mentioned groups will be expected to reinforce the newly recovering person's negative feelings. A rapid course of action in getting the person connected to the support of a self-help group, and involvement with carefully selected recovery supporters from among old friends and family, are helpful in countering negative influences.

d.   Subtle and extended efforts are best suited for resolving other emotion arousing recovery issues. Addressing such issues as teaching opportunities present themselves is a rational approach. Among such issues are: guiding the person to accept responsibility for themselves totally, ceasing blaming, alibiing, accusing, taking his own heat; ceasing victim-type behavior and thinking, and other manipulative games aimed at controlling others; and the change of thinking from an external locus of control to an internal locus of control.

Enlisting the involvement and assistance of other treatment group persons when working to resolve these and other issues is perhaps the most helpful resource the counselor has. In the entire treatment process of Stage I, keep paramount the principles of recovery progressiveness, and first things first.

Chapter VII

ABSTINENCE IN CD TREATMENT AND RECOVERY

The issue of abstinence-based CD treatment versus treatment aimed at returning the CD client to moderate social alcohol use or drug use continues to rear its head and deserves some expanded comments. There may be some confirmed chemically dependent people who have returned to substance use at a predictable level that does not result in dysfunction or destruction. I don't know any of them, and I assume their number must be infinitesimally small.

I have known few who did not try it at least once and either quickly sought abstinence again or regressed to an addictive level of use. Unfortunately, there are some of the latter who were never able to achieve abstinence again after relapse. There are no known claims of a means of predicting which CD person can safely become a drinking alcoholic, and which ones cannot, if such is possible at all.

Abstinence is a condition required to arrive at a state of treatability and to preserve the state of recovery. Many writers seem incorrectly to presume abstinence to be the primary, and even conclusive, goal of CD treatment. CD treatment is not to cure the CD person's "sin" of using alcohol or drugs by getting him to give up drinking and using.

There have been a number of published reports of research intended to demonstrate the feasibility of treatment methods that would result in CD recovery without abstaining from alcohol. Such research has ranged from a variety of behavior modification using aversive techniques to pharmacology. These efforts will no doubt continue, and well they should. So far, long-range follow-ups of the subjects of such research have not proven conclusively successful or have failed completely.

A noted and much discussed research of about 1970 used aversion techniques to teach 20 alcoholics how to drink moderately, that is, to be social drinkers. A ten year follow-up of 19 of the 20 men (one was not located) found that 13 of them (65%) were rehospitalized within the first year, and within five years more than 80% had required further treatment. Four of the 20 were dead, two being found drowned with high BALs (blood alcohol levels). Eight continued to drink excessively throughout the long-term. All had one or more of the following alcohol related consequences during the follow-up period: job loss, arrest, marital break up, and hospitalizations for alcoholism and related physical illness. Six were abstaining totally from drinking, having independently decided that abstinence was the only way they could avoid alcohol related problems.

The overwhelming weight of evidence must say to us that alcoholics who have achieved recovery from their drug dependency cannot and should not ever drink again. A respected professional in the addiction field (Miller, N. S., 1995) refers to the research cited above as an illusion that increasing alcoholics' awareness of internal cues of blood alcohol levels would facilitate their return to asymptomatic drinking.

Abstinence alone is not recovery. Abstinence is necessary for recovery at the present level of knowledge. Abstinence and learning about addiction begins the first step, the beginning of recovery. Abstinence does not automatically give the CD person a happy life. Abstinence may get the CD out of a bad place, but getting out of a bad place just gets you out. That alone will not transport the CD to a good place in her life. Abstinence is like standing at the starting line. The race hasn't started yet, but at least the CD is standing up and ready to go.

AA's 12 steps are meant to be the CD's road map to recovery. The CD must decide where the treatment and the 12 steps are to take her. There is a personal element to the definition of recovery. The individual will decide how far he wants to go, and what he wants to change. The person who wants only to quit drinking or using needs only detoxification, not treatment. If he wants recovery, it can include peace of mind, liking himself, getting control of his life, and rejoining the human race. He must undertake a self-propelled journey that will probably affect every facet of his being and continue for a lifetime. Recovering is not something you just do, such as becoming abstinent or even performing all the suggested treatment tasks (See the comments on The Compliant Client.) Recovering is what one becomes. Recovering is changing, achieved by recovery tasks that become a part of the CD's life.

How does the committed CD go about building behaviors and defenses that make abstinence from alcohol and drugs possible?

a. Stay out of drinking and using places.

b. Avoid drinking/using partners.

c. Remove all alcohol and drugs from the house.

d. Get rid of drug paraphernalia.

e. Get rid of CDs, tapes, pictures, literature, and other trigger items associated with drinking/using.

f. Move away from the neighborhood if there is widespread alcohol or drug abuse or trafficking going on there.

g. Follow different routes to work, school, shopping, or other frequented places as necessary to avoid passing by or near drinking/using locations.

h. Get rid of cash cards or ATM cards.

i. Identify and avoid other 'triggers' to craving or to drug-seeking behavior.

j. Maintain close contact with and actively use personal support group.

There is no assurance of successful recovery from alcoholism or other chemical dependencies without abstinence from mind-altering drugs. Therefore, the basis for any discussion of counseling theory or approaches and techniques for use in counseling chemically dependent people must assume a commitment to abstinence by the patient or client. While I believe that this view is agreed upon by the vast majority of professionals with extended experience in the chemical dependence field, it is also well known that many members of the mental health community who see alcoholics and other drug dependent people in their practices deny this reality or rationalize exceptions to the principle. Many counselors in the field, especially those who have struggled through recovery themselves, strongly believe the need for abstinence but find themselves hard pressed to explain to clients in logical terms why it is so.

A major breakthrough has been made through the educational efforts of Dr. David Ohlms and others. His lectures and educational films represent the forefront of accumulated research in the alcoholism field, and help to explain some of the mysteries of the illness. Subsequent research now points to similar metabolic/biochemical processes related to the susceptibility to dependence on other psychoactive drugs.

Treatment of an illness is aimed at improving function. In the treatment of chemical dependence, abstinence is not an aim but a means to an end, wih the end being the improved function of the client. The achievement of abstinence, the basic condition for an improvement of function, that is to say recovery, is often extremely difficult because of the physiological effect that psychoactive substances have on the alcoholic/addicted person. Many substances, the "drugs of choice" and many of the usually beneficial ones, can trigger in the CD person the physiological reactions that gave rise to the addiction susceptibility to begin with. At the present time there is no known "cure" for this biological susceptibility that would allow the resumption of the safe use of psychoactive substances. No rational person would suggest that it would be safe for the recovering heroin addict to do a little skin-popping of "H" on the weekends, or that the cocaine addict could stay straight by only snorting an occasional line or two at social gatherings. By the same reasoning, the alcoholic is not at all likely to maintain his recovery while attempting to practice "social drinking."

The physiological susceptibility to chemical dependence makes an important part of the educational component of treatment and awareness by the CD client that medications that have any potential for addiction or dependence should be prescribed only as necessary. The client should advise his physicians that he is recovering from alcoholism or other drug addiction, if the physician is not already aware of it.

A psychiatric or other medical disorder that co-exists with chemical dependence and which requires a psychotropic medication for its treatment demands an exception to the strict abstinence rule. The fully abstinent recovering person must be helped to understand why the exception is necessary for the CD person with a psychiatric disorder. Unfortunately, there are many who suffer with such dual diagnoses. About 15% of CD persons are in this dual problem group, approximately the same percentage as in the general population. For them treatment of both conditions is complicated, making recovery from either an especially difficult task. Treatment of the dual diagnosed client should be a joint endeavor of both mental health and substance abuse professionals, or by an individual professionally trained in both fields.

Recovering CD clients should also be made aware of the phenomenon of state-dependent learning. Both animal and human studies have shown that learning that occurred in either a drugged state or a non-drugged state would score higher when tested for recall in the same mental state in which the learning took place, or score lower when tested in a mental state different than the one in which the learning occurred. Applied to the process of treating CD clients, we can assume that the person who has learned the ways of maintaining sobriety while in a non-drugged (drug free) state will have poorer access to that learning while he is in a drugged state. In other words the non-abstinent alcoholic or drug-addict is incapable of fully practicing the recovery skills he learned while drug-free in a treatment program. Conversely, the client who goes through treatment without being drug-free will not have learned in an accessible way recovery skills and lessons when the state of abstinence is desired (Klein, 1987).

James E. Royce, in his *Alcohol problems & alcoholism: A Comprehensive survey (Revised Edition)*, 1989, summarizes the major research on the question "Can Recovered Alcoholics be Conditioned to Drink Socially?" The conclusion, of course, is a clear No, they cannot. The most thorough research (Helzer et al., 1985, reported by Miller. N., 1995) studied five-year and seven-year outcomes on 1,289 diagnosed and treated alcoholics, and found only 1.6% were successful moderate drinkers. Of this tiny fraction, most were female and who all showed few clear symptoms of true alcoholism. "In any case, it would be unethical to suggest to any patient a goal with a failure rate of 98.4 percent." (p.134)

For those who ask for help but refuse to accept the need for total abstinence, challenge them with Marty Mann's self-test to determine their level of alcoholism. It requires that a person limit drinking to a maximum of three single drinks on any day during a six month period. Choosing not to drink on any particular day is permissible, but if he drinks more than three drinks on a single day during the six months, he should be considered alcoholic. Mann assumed that a genuine alcoholic would lose control at some time during the period and drink more than he intended. Metzger (1988, p.164), in describing the test, noted that it may be effective only with gamma alcoholics and fail to catch other types of alcoholics who never lose control of their drinking. He offers another method which may lead to acceptance of abstinence rather than giving in to the wish for treatment with modification of drinking as a goal.

The early stage alcoholic who insists that help to moderate drinking is all that is necessary, and who has no wish to quit completely, is probably not ready to make other changes for a full-blown recovery goal. For this client, Metzger (pp 165-169) recommends a paradoxical technique called charting, that appears to be for the purpose of helping the client achieve a modified drinking goal, while actually aimed at abstinence. The charting technique avoids confrontation by the counselor; instead the client is brought face to face with her own drinking pattern. While educating the client about potential substance abuse dependence and about strategies to avoid it, the counselor addresses the issues that are or may be affected by problem substance use.

The charting exercise is started by asking the client to contract for a goal of modified use and to chart on a graph the days and amounts of use. The goal of a daily drinking limit, a reduction of typical usage, for a month or so is agreed upon. Following achievement of that goal, the next goal is set to limit use to every other day. When this goal has been reached by the client, the goal is advanced to a schedule of two days of abstinence followed by one day of reduced drinking. Episodes of excessive drinking on drinking days or failing to abstain on no-drinking days should be thoroughly discussed with the client - What triggered it? Why did the client choose to drink?

The charting technique may have three possible outcomes: the client modifies drinking to one or two single drinks twice a week; the client decides to stop drinking entirely, or he fails to keep the charting contract and over-drinks on a continuing basis. The first two possibilities may be considered successful treatment outcomes. The third one would hopefully prove to the client his out-of-control state and a need for total abstinence.

Abstinence from all psychoactive drugs as a necessity to the successful recovery from chemical dependency should not be compromised. If you, the reader, is unconvinced of this truth, or if you are toying with the idea that a treatment goal of "cutting down" is valid, you are referred to the writings of James Milam, Kinney and Leaton, Norman Miller, Lawrence Metzger, or any of the other respected researchers or therapists in the substance abuse field.

Chapter VIII

THE "SHEEP DIP" PRESUMPTION

The sheep dip presumption: The belief that the exposure of the addicted person to a presumed therapeutic milieu for some period of time constitutes "treatment" and, if the milieu is potent enough, "cure" will result. Many addicts and many others in our society believe the sheep dip presumption to be real.

Recovery from alcoholism or other drug addiction requires work and dedication. Recovery requires that both small and major changes be made in most areas of the addicted person's life. The Serenity Prayer reminds us of a basic change process - "courage to change the things I can (change) and the wisdom to know the difference (between that which is changeable and that which is not changeable)." The recovering person must not only recognize what needs to be and can be changed, but also that only she is the change agent for herself; i.e., she must actually do the changing. It doesn't mean to just show up for group or the AA meetings and things will change automatically. Recovery is not a passive activity. It requires the wholehearted involvement of the addicted person. In other words, chemical dependence treatment is not like dipping sheep for ticks - wading in at one end infested and coming out the other end clean - with the sheep exerting no effort other than allowing herself to be driven (coerced or enticed) through the tank.

Fortunately for the counselor, all clients don't enter treatment expecting to have something (recovery?) done to them. However, many do so. After all, addictive thinking harbors the belief that something external must be the source of relief, happiness, health, improved functioning, and/or the solution to life's problems. One of our tasks as counselors is to be aware of the client's perceived locus of control. The person with an external control orientation accepts little or no responsibility for the course of his life, good or bad. he often feels powerless to determine or carry out changes in his life. He often quickly directs blame toward others for everything that goes wrong in his life.

An internal locus of control means an acceptance of responsibility for what happens in his life, how he copes with reality, and what choices he makes. It also includes a recognition of his own inner strengths and weaknesses. This outlook on life and perception of oneself is a positive one. Do not confuse it with the addictive thinking that leads the addict/alcoholic to believe that he should be able to control the people and events of the world around him (including alcohol and drugs). The addict often suffers from the delusion that others are to blame for all his problems and others must be responsible for getting him well.

The "sheep dip" perception of treatment is an example of the addictive thinking that reflects the external locus of control. It rationalizes onto others the success or failure of his treatment. Haven't we all heard, or even uttered it ourselves at times, "I went to (AA or X Treatment Program) a few times and it didn't do a thing for me."

The "sheep dip" expectation of treatment may be altered with heavy emphasis early in treatment on completion of tasks of change that only the client can achieve. This category of tasks includes doing what must be done to clean up his environment of alcohol and drugs, behavioral changes involving elimination of social contacts with fellow drinkers and users, and beginning a rigorous involvement in a 12-step mutual-help fellowship.

The CD counselor should be careful not to give his charges the idea that because he, the counselor, is the leader of the band, he is also the player of all the instruments. Or to use the sheep dip analogy, the counselor should not allow the impression that all the client needs to do to recover is to passively allow himself to be led through the treatment "dip" and he will be all better. And if it doesn't turn out that way, it won't be his fault - yeah, right!

Some sheep dip treatment approaches that are erroneously believed by some to be effective upon external application are: TLC (alone), guilt, punishment, isolation, physical control, shame, prescribed medication, electric shock, hydrotherapy, hypnosis, and other treatment programs that fail to require active, change-evoking involvement of the client. Aversion therapies and covert sensitization may have some short-term positive results, but seem to require prolonged reinforcement sessions and the support of a self-help group. Use of such external approaches to treatment could leave the client with the belief that there is someone or something to blame should he relapse.

Recovery from the addiction is the means of escaping its influence on the addicted person's life. Abstinence from psychoactive substances is required to keep it that way. "Just quitting" is like dipping the sheep to rid it of ticks. The sheep-dip treatment method works for sheep just as being momentarily clean and dry works for the addict. The sheep that is successfully rid of its infestation, when exposed to ticks again, will become infested again. After all, the dip method only affects the surface; it doesn't change the environment which may never be totally free of ticks.

Just only to quit using is not treatment. Nothing is really different except that the surface may look better for a while. Unlike the tick infested sheep, the addicted person has the potential to determine the state of his internal environment. He can choose to make changes including decisions that will lead to regaining control of his own life - new thoughts, new feelings, and new behaviors.

Chapter IX

CHANGE

Chemically dependent or not, we are responsible for what happens in our lives, perhaps except for wars or epidemics of disease. However, the alcoholic's disease causes him to think, feel and act in ways that say he should not be held responsible for his actions. Not true of course, but we must look deeper for the point where responsibility begins.

The disease of chemical dependence results from a union of an addictive substance and a susceptible host. The chemically dependent person is not to blame for his suscep-tibility, but he must be responsible for ingesting the addictive substance which is the catalyst that activates the disease that comes to control the addict's emotions, thoughts and deeds. For the ensuing disease-related state to continue managing the life of the victim it must continue to be fed the substance or a substitute by the victim.

The victim also must be responsible for getting treatment, that is to say the help necessary for change to occur. Resistance to the craving for the substance and to changing the compulsive behaviors, irrational thinking and the unwanted feelings will not occur until the use of the addictive chemical substance ceases. No one but the chemically dependent person can bring the use of the substance to a meaningful halt.

An overly simplified formula for chemical dependence recovery might read like this: Stop using and give up related behaviors. Easier said than done, of course. Each of the two parts of the simplified recovery formula presents mountainous complexities, and of course the process of recovery does not stop there. Many changes need to be made which brings us to the subject of this chapter - change. A treatment strategy that can maximize recovery potential must involve the client in the change process. The counselor's role is to assist the recovering person to achieve abstinence and to understand and cope with that change process.

The full-blown alcoholic or drug addict, unless also a sociopath, is almost always afflicted with a troubled self-image and a low self-confidence that have resulted from disasters the addictive behaviors have left behind: Lies, broken promises, failed responsibilities, hurt loved ones, deceit, selfishness, fears, self-destruction, self-deception, self-doubt, pretense, losses without number. Beneath the chemically dependent person's defenses of grandiosity, arrogance, apathy, and denial hide senses of shame, failure, uselessness, hopelessness, guilt, remorse, and shattered ego.

The presence of distorted emotions in the substance abuse counselor's clients invites addressing them directly in unnecessary therapy. Reinforcing the bases for abstinent behavior and bringing into awareness the disease-related thoughts and behaviors provides the CD client the means for self-change. The use of shame and embarrassment over the substance influenced behavior is a sort of blackmail to keep the client in treatment and is not recommended. The counselor of the alcoholic/addict in early (Stage I) treatment should not yield to the temptation to address self-image and self-confidence problems as the primary treatment strategy, no matter how enticing. Some behavioral and environmental change goals will occur spontaneously with the successful achievement of abstinence.

First and foremost, these changes will help to establish and maintain abstinence from psychoactive substances, allowing the client to experience a new or renewed positive self-image and self-confidence. As recovery advances, the issues of restitution, forgiveness, amends, and other self-image problems can be raised without overly-stressing a still fragile ego.

Issues of self which have not yet remitted following the achievement of abstinence and have resisted necessary progress from indirect intervention of CD counseling may require time-limited specific work. Unless the condition of abstinence can be firmly established, such specific counseling efforts are likely to be futile and will certainly delay other goal achievements. Attempting to resolve guilt, for example, while the client continues involved in the guilt producing behaviors, will not succeed.

The first behavioral change must be the cessation of alcohol and drug use. Inextricably tied to chemical use are the use-related persons, places, things, ideas, and values.

Behavioral changes, such as avoiding the people, places and things that make up the pattern of the chemical dependency lifestyle, must go hand in hand with abstinence. Where one thing is taken away, another must take its place, or the vacuum will encourage a return of the behavior, including the substance use. The new behavior will involve developing new support system elements and introducing sobriety-compatible behaviors that will further advance recovery by allowing the client to see himself in a new light and as a new person.

In the treatment of chemical dependence, recovery is accomplished by change. Recovery requires the surrendering, the giving up, of certain behaviors, lifestyles, and ways of thinking and feeling. It further requires the taking up and adoption of new and equivalent behaviors. In other words we are working deliberately to bring about the substitution of one behavior, lifestyle, and pattern of thinking and feeling for another. This is the process called change without which there can be no real recovery.

Both aspects of the change process are necessary to be effective and lasting because nature abhors a vacuum. Quitting something or giving up something without choosing a new "some-thing" to take its place, will leave a void that will attract a replacement that has the attractiveness of a painless substitute. Conversely, trying to take on a new behavior, lifestyle, thought process, or habitual feeling, without having to give up the old way obviously will not work.

Another law of physics also applies: two bodies of matter cannot occupy the same space simultaneously. In other words the person wanting to change cannot have it both ways. This doctrine of change is true in all aspects of life, but is so disastrously displayed when the addict/alcoholic relapses. As our clients struggle to change, help them to see that as much effort is called for in adding the new as it is in giving up the old.

At first sight, the optional new alternatives often seem like bad news to the novice recovering addict: non-stop AA, adopting boring pastimes, associating with dull party-poopers, doing without the chemical magic to feeling good. It is safe to say that most newcomers harbor the idea that it is possible to get clean and sober without giving up all their old haunts, old friends, and old activities that are associated with using. As a result, the second part of change, the adding of new behaviors, new lifestyles, new ways of thinking, and new feeling needs, is harder to accept.

Change or the anticipation of change produces anxiety. When we find our lives in a turmoil with things not turning out as we wanted, it appears to be human nature to look first outside ourselves to the environment for the cause of our problems. We may blame others and project our frustration, anger or resentment onto others. We seem unable to put two and two together, or to recognize the relationship between what we think and do and what is transpiring in our lives. In short we deny our own responsibility for how life is going. We keep trying to make the old way work even after repeated failures. Even while a person's life is going down hill as the result of something that is obvious to others around him, he may be unable or unwilling to see the need for his personal change.

There are at least three ways that unwanted, disruptive, or ineffective, self-defeating, but changeable, thinking, feeling or behaving may have originated. It seems necessary to recognize these sources when attempting to analyze the dynamics, processes and need of change.

First, there are unwanted and harmful events in people's lives over which they have no direct part in causing, or over which they have no control. Examples are natural disasters, wars, the behaviors of others, and most inherited physiology. In most of these instances the ability to change what can be changed and to accept and cope with that which cannot is required in order to stabilize our lives. Even learning to cope may require a change in how we think, feel or act.

At the opposite end of the change spectrum is the person who is so fearful of making a mistake, of doing something wrong, that his journey through life is a constant walking on eggshells. That individual may be so cautious that he is unable to make a decision for fear it will be wrong, and is afraid to take a risk of any proportion. This person, too, is a prospect for a manner of change - learning when and how to take a risk. This person has been scripted to believe that perfection is his only option but lacks the self-confidence to achieve it.

A third barrier to change that frequently can be problematic in our lives springs from faulty beliefs learned as biases and inaccuracies heard or observed in childhood. These distortions are accepted as reality, and they become the rules by which our lives are run. Chemical substances give the CD person a false sense of coping with frustration over those things he cannot control, over-concern for how he is accepted by others, and fears of every kind.

A common effect of a substance dependent lifestyle is the dysfunctional ways of interacting with others necessary to the maintenance of the illness. They are behaviors that are often exaggerated and entrenched, and accompanied by a declining self-image. In the face of the CD person's task of starting on the road to recovery, it is easy to be diverted by an attempt to work at changing all the troublesome thinking, feelings and behaviors.

Counselors know that many changes are necessary to getting the chemically dependent person reentered into normal society. The counselor and the client should carefully review and jointly decide what changes are immediately necessary for him to get clean and sober and to learn the means of directing his own long-term recovery. In setting change goals for Stage I CD treatment, less is better.

Recently a young woman client was lamenting to me how her life had been a series of problems, troubles, and disasters for the past nine of her twenty-one years.

"I always screw things up," she said. "I don't know how to make things different, I am afraid."

She was just beginning to admit the harmful effects of alcohol and other drugs on her life. She was just learning that dishonesty and irresponsibility are also root causes of fractured relationships and a shattered self-image. We ask,

"Why doesn't she just change?" And, "What are her pressing treatment needs?"

The first goal is to get clean and sober. Next she must structure her environment to be the safest possible, by eliminating or drastically reducing opportunities or temptations to drink or use. It is much more important to make the changes required to avoid those people who create stress or other emotional discomfort than it is to change relationship patterns with them in the period of early recovery.

Thought processes, emotional states, and behavioral reactions due to a negative self-image, a distorted world view, or an irrational set of values, are justifiably a secondary priority to building time clean and sober, and learning those things necessary to avoiding relapse. The addicted person has lost a large amount of her ability to make rational choices or to persevere in recovery efforts. Guidance and support are usually required for most persons to make recovery a reality by choosing and addressing only essential goals.

To change means "to alter or modify something." Changing implies taking what is and transforming or converting it into something different. It is exchanging one thing for another. The changing required for recovery from chemical dependence must follow the definition of replacing the disruptive or undesirable element with a healthy one. A broad case-in-point is the exchanging of an addictive lifestyle for a socially normal one. Viewing change as just quitting, just giving it up, won't work for long if at all. The counselor's challenge is to lead his client in finding and adopting satisfying alternative ideas, values, and behaviors compatible with an abstinent lifestyle.

We humans have a need for predictability. We want to know how things are going to turn out. We want things to be tomorrow as they were today. We have a need to know that stimulus A will produce response B - even if that outcome is painful. Most people, yes, probably even you and

I, fear or distrust that which is different in our daily lives. As irrational as it may sound, most of us would rather suffer with familiar pain than to risk the unknown of change.

The need for predictability is so universal and seems so strong that it might be considered a basic human drive or motivator. This inclination to be locked into particular behaviors exists, even if it produces painful consequences, as long as the consequences are predictable. Even when we recognize that change is necessary for our very survival, change is hard, change is resisted.

When we do change our own behaviors, attitudes or beliefs, unexpected results ensue. People react to us differently experiencing anxiety due to our change. In some ways, we become strangers to ourselves and to others. In other words we have become unpredictable (temporarily) to the people close to us. We don't respond as we once did and that makes those people anxious. At least at first, both subtly and not so subtly, the behavior or reaction of friends and family to even positive change will tend to push one back into the old predictable behavior. Our own subconscious mind may become a party to this conspiracy. It is very important that the person working to change unwanted behaviors recognizes that this unwitting tendency of those closest and most supportive of his efforts to change may unconsciously set booby traps in his pathway to change. Not only our own fears of the unknown, but the fears of the people around us make change difficult.

For the CD person the only chance for a fulfilling, meaningful life is change - usually numerous changes. Not only have they to struggle against powerful dynamics in themselves and others that resist change, they have also to contend with a biochemical predisposition to metabolize mood- or mind-altering drugs in a harmful way, and with both positive and negative conditioning to the effects of the addictive qualities of one or more drugs.

Keeping in mind how difficult it is for non-addicted people to make life changes, it is easier to understand how much more difficult it is for the addict or alcoholic to change so drastically. The dynamic of change isn't any different for the addicted person than for those who are not addicted to a substance, only harder.

Unfortunately, the motivation for change usually springs from having reached such a level of pain or fear through the old way of doing things that one can no longer ignore or deny what is being done to themselves and are ready to put it away in exchange for something new. It means being sick and tired of being sick and tired (Phil Larsen).

The CD client may desperately work to hold onto the old while taking on the new, but it won't work. He must choose! Is he willing to let the old die - to put it into the past? It is only in this way that he can possess a new and better life.

In theory, we can change in an instant those things available to change. In practice however, it takes a much longer time for the new way to become a real part of us - 3 to 6 years or more for the recovering addict or alcoholic. A great investment in energy and awareness is demanded to resist sliding back to the old way or relapsing. The desire for the new must be encouraged and reinforced. The memory of the old painful way must be preserved. As counselors, we must admonish our clients to not forget how bad it once was. The tendency for a memory of the wonderful first effects of chemical use remains deep within the alcoholic/addict, sometimes for life.

Finally, if the commitment is strong and long-term, the new way will become a part of oneself - not just a seemingly unattainable wish, but a reality. We counselors are in truth powerless to bring about change in someone else. A major principle in regard to change is: "We cannot change anyone but ourselves."

We can be a model to others.

We can offer support to others.

We can teach others ways of learning to change.

We can have hopes and wishes for others.

But, like it or not! The choice to change is theirs.

Conversely, we cannot expect others to change us. We must do it ourselves - usually with help from others - but we cannot honestly blame others when our own lives remain in the old rut. There is another dynamic of relationships which can hinder change. This is called enabling, which is:

Doing for someone that which he can do for himself.

Assuming someone else's responsibilities.

Covering for him. Protecting him from the consequences of his behavior.

Being the constant fixer or caretaker.

Denying him the opportunities to make mistakes and grow from the experience.

Trying to force change by nagging, manipulation, or guilt.

Withholding from him your encouragement and belief in his ability to change.

The Serenity Prayer says it in a nutshell: "God, grant me the serenity to accept the things I cannot change, the courage to change the things I can, and the wisdom to know the difference." (Reinhold Niebuhr).

In the context of desired change via counseling or psychotherapy, there is the perennial search (or fantasy) by therapists to discover and apply a technique of instant cure. Short-term therapy has evolved into a formalized brief-therapy, or coaching which in turn has encouraged some to believe in the possibility of a one-session cure.

Certainly, the diagnostic and treatment skills of the counselor are of paramount importance to the outcome of the treatment effort. We must agree that a skillful and experienced counselor would possess the means to bring the client most quickly to the resolution of the troublesome problem. However, the counselor is not the principal member of the treatment effort. To fail to place the client as the principal performer in the treatment process is to deny the power of the client's role in its outcome. A counselor-centered view of the treatment process implies an omnipotence that exceeds reality. The client has the ability to frustrate, defeat, circumvent, block, undermine, or withdraw from the efforts of the most astute therapist. Despite a recognition of the values inherent in having the counselor be the authority, to dominate the process, it is the client who makes the decision whether the counselor will be the leader in more than a superficial sense. The client has the final say, whether we like it or not and whether the counselor's opinion is in his best interest or not.

We cannot make a client get well in opposition to his wishes. We can decide that the client doesn't know what is best for himself, but we are not able to make him do what we think is best. We, the counselors, may be in nominal charge of the session (and ideally we should be), but the only thing we can do with our clients unilaterally is to refuse to work with them. With everything else that goes on in the counseling session, the client makes the final decision by virtue of his cooperation, resistance, and other factors influencing his readiness to change or do "work".

In light of the above, we say, "Meet the client where he is." The good news seems to be that at some level most clients will at some time be ready to make changes that they already know they need to make. There is a time for all things, including a time for growing. If the time is right, if the situation is right, the time for growth may be influenced. This is the teachable moment. This is that elusive moment when the client is ready to hear and able to internalize what is heard. It is the time and circumstance that come together to clear away the client's lack of readiness or trust in what he has known all along - what must be done to get well.

Once, early in my counseling career, I chanced to encounter "John", a former client, while shopping in a local mall. In such circumstances I allow the former client to choose whether to speak to his counselor in public. But John greeted me warmly and proceeded to give me an update of his life situation since we had talked last. He was doing well and appeared happy in his successful sobriety.

"Ed," he said, "I will never forget what you said to me one day in group. It really hit home, and I think it turned my whole life around."

Wow, I thought, *I must have lucked upon the magical formula for making alcoholics recover.* I wondered what wisdom I had imparted at that moment that had produced such profound results. I asked John to remind me of the content of that momentous interaction.

"I was telling the group some hard-luck story," John told me, "in which I had paid what I thought was an unfairly harsh penalty, and you said to me, 'John, we must pay the consequences of our own behavior.' That hit me like a ton of bricks, and I have never forgotten it."

Not only did I not remember the specific incident John referred to, I knew I must have uttered those words or their equivalent numerous times to virtually every client I ever had, and most of the time they were shrugged off as the trite cliché they are and with no discernible effect one way or another. Why had they produced such seeming impact on John? I don't for a minute believe that there was anything magical about those particular words, as important as they are, neither then nor now. I do believe that by some fortunate quirk of chance the words were uttered at the time John was able to hear them in a way that was to him motivation to change. He heard at that precise teachable moment what he certainly already knew, the words that reminded him of their value in managing his own life.

Since that day I have made a studied effort to recognize those moments of readiness and in turn be ready to take the most beneficial advantage of them. Sometimes I succeed and sometimes I fail to recognize a specific teachable moment, and I continue to be pleasantly surprised when a former client thanks me for a turning point that mostly he or she deserves the credit for. There are really no magic words, only ready clients. We counselors owe it to them to be ready to enhance their moments of learning.

Techniques That May Help a Person to Accomplish Change

Approaches to change address one or more aspects of the cognitive, affective, behavioral paradigm. People can and do make changes on getting new information or new evidence if their cognition in the problem area is not distorted by faulty reasoning. The person with his reason intact may change thought, feeling or behavior based on previously unknown facts, such as research findings, or discovering a more logical perception of information he already has. Unimpaired reason will usually result in change due to new experiences. A functional Adult Ego State (Eric Berne's Transactional Analysis) has the capacity to solve problems, make probability estimates, and perceive the consequences of thoughts, feelings or actions.

Realistically, few of the chemically dependent clients we see are currently endowed with an Adult completely uncontaminated by biases, inaccurate data, the physiological effects of mind altering drugs, or emotional crises.

The counselor may shorten the change process by discovering the cognitive impairments of her client, and tailor interventions aimed at change to coincide with the functional part of the Adult Ego State. For example, the teaching of knowledge related to alcohol and other drug addiction may require more than straightforward presentation of the facts in lecture form. Demonstrations or the analysis of the client's own experiences may be needed for understanding to occur.

When the logic of the necessity for abstinence does not penetrate the client's denial defenses, a contract required of him to abstain as a condition of staying in the recovery program may keep him focused until reason returns. This tactic is most effective when completion of treatment is required to avoid an unwanted consequence such as loss of child custody, losing a job, or doing jail time. Coercion is justified in the face of the reality that sound judgment, the ability to make beneficial decisions, is out of reach of the newly abstinent addict.

Whatever is legal and humane should be considered for use to allow the clearing of the mental fog over the time necessary for the client to regain his reasoning ability. Genuine change will only occur when given the drug-free time necessary for the person's faculties to regain some normalcy. The passage of time free of drug use in itself usually will result in some positive changes. It is necessary to do change-producing tasks.

The client committed to recovery and ready to make the necessary changes may be ready for dealing with issues in the affective arena. It seems to be a given that many alcoholics and drug addicts have lost touch with their more sensitive emotions. It is also true that the alcoholic/addict is often awash in negative and hidden self-blaming emotions such as guilt, despair, resentment, anger, etc. My personal conviction is that the so-called "feelings group" is out of place for the newly abstinent CD client. Instead, the instillation of hope for a better life, a belief that recovery is possible for him, and the resurrection of positive feelings about himself are more productive.

Later in the progression of recovery, a personal confrontation with feelings, such as dealt with in the AA Step Four, will be more meaningful. In the meantime, encourage the client to "act as if" his emotions are intact, "act as if" he fully understands what is being said in the treatment process. The sequence of thought, feeling, and action can often be made to work in reverse, that is, behaving on faith can be followed by an altered emotional experience and, at last a new understanding.

An essential issue to resolve with the chemically dependent client is what he wants and expects from "recovery" or "treatment". Be specific. How will he recognize it when it has been achieved? How will he know when he has arrived? How will others know he is recovering? A simplistic reality is that if you don't know where you are going, how will you know which direction to take or know when you have arrived?

Change, of course, involves choosing. The client may very likely have lost the habit of making thought-out choices; instead he just reacts to undisciplined emotions and the physical demands of the addiction. It must be recognized early on in the recovery process that the addict/alcoholic's life has become unmanageable. Regaining control will be recognized by beginning to make rational choices again.

The conditions necessary for change are offered by L'Abate (1997, pp 40-66). These conditions include: admitting the existence of the problem(s); accepting help in the change process; receiving positive, effective help; having hope that change is possible; and regaining or establishing a sense of control. Filling the role of the helper in the change process, the counselor must win the confidence of the client. The ability of the counselor to establish rapport with her clients, even those that are unlikable, requires advanced counseling skills as well as empathy.

The client's role in the change process is to actually put the changes into practice. Commitments to make the changes may be encouraged by providing reinforcing reward such as positive recognition for compliance in practicing the committed behavior, and by appropriate consequences for non-compliance. Assigning each client to a "buddy", another client who has made good recovery progress, is such a strategy. AA's sponsor system makes use of this method in making change possible. Having the client put his commitments in writing is another.

An early essential task for the outpatient chemically dependent client is evaluating his living and working environments, and taking the actions necessary to assure that these places are safety zones, free of alcohol and other drugs, free of dealers and users, and populated by people who are supportive to his recovery efforts. Persons receiving treatment in either inpatient or residential facilities are often unable to make decisions affecting his home or work environments until discharged. Unless staff and/or family cooperate in getting necessary changes made prior to discharge from treatment, the client may be returning to environments that are hazardous to his recovery efforts.

Equally important in removing or minimizing the risks in our drug-oriented society is a detailed plan to avoid places, people and things that are associated with the client's drinking or drug using. This phase of neutralizing the environment may include plotting new routes to and from work, AA or NA meetings, shopping, and leisure activities. These and other restructuring of activities should be recorded in a treatment plan and monitored for compliance. Enlist the cooperation of a supportive family member, friend, or a treatment "buddy" to accompany the recovering client in travel or activities which may encounter triggers to relapse thinking or behavior.

Many changes are usually necessary in the life of the newly recovering person. Caution should be taken that there are no demands for change that are not essential to the recovery process. Expecting the client to make changes that defy the logic of need is likely to backfire and result in increased resistance and the loss of cooperation with the treatment goals. Counselors must be particularly careful that their personal biases do not result in burdening the change agenda of the already stressed client.

The practical common sense of behavioral changes and avoidance of risky environments set the stage for the client to reshape his self-image positively and increase his self-confidence without the emotional stress of digging into past history or the confrontational insight psychotherapies. A bare minimum of one year of stable sobriety and recovery work is recommended to prepare the recovering chemically dependent for any necessary heavy mental or emotional therapy.

Changes in the external environment are not for the purpose of delineating what is right or wrong, good or bad, but as secondary to changing some structures related to lifestyle, self-esteem, self-confidence, and to impart grounds for belief in the change process. Potent changes are those that reveal to the client activities, pursuits, goals, and meaningful experiences that feel good and contribute to the building of a new, positive self-image.

Chapter X

CHEMICAL DEPENDENCY TREATMENT

Treatment Stage I

Abstinence is entirely within the province of the chemically dependent client. No one can enforce abstinence from psychoactive substances by the addicted/dependent person for the long term. The desire to be well must rest in the victim of the illness.

Short term abstinence can be enforced fairly successfully while the person is an inmate in a closely regulated hospital or residential treatment facility for the term of the residency. In today's HMO controlled health care, chemical dependence treatment is very unlikely to occur in these environments, or at most only during a brief period of detoxification. In the outpatient setting, control of the client's actions is limited to the relatively brief time she is present in the outpatient program's facility. The majority of the outpatient's time is her own and abstinence is her constant choice. This condition is not bad. In fact, the outpatient has the opportunity to win daily victories over the cravings and compulsive urges by making abstinence-related choices. She does not usually have such self-confidence building opportunities while in the hospital.

It is a sound assumption that the outpatient client who has succeeded in making some changes in his behaviors and learned to use some strategies to avoid slips and relapses is farther ahead in recovery progress than the person whose abstinence has been physically enforced. It is necessary to interject at this point that there are those who are not capable of maintaining abstinence while being faced with the opportunities and temptations of our drug oriented society. We all know of late-stage, seemingly untreatable alcoholics and addicts who, after numerous enforced detoxifications, have found the hope and the courage to overcome their disease and find sobriety. However, do not let anyone convince you that outpatient substance abuse treatment is an inferior treatment method.

The primary approach to treatment of substance abuse is encompassed in strategies designed to help the client succeed in becoming free of alcohol and drugs and give him the incentives and tools to stay that way - if he continues to choose to do so. The counselor is actually able to do no more. What, in a practical sense, is the substance abuse counselor's responsibility in the treatment of her clients in stage one of recovery?

The process should be based upon the thorough assessment of the client and a determination of the existence of physical, psychological, or social crises, and the status of current alcohol and drug use. Crises need to be addressed first, by enlisting the help of community resources, and by guidance of the client in personal efforts. The barriers to the person's full attention to the recovery effort must be removed or at least alleviated to allow him to put his attention primarily on recovery tasks. Obviously others beside the primary counselor are likely to be working with the client. When these preparatory functions have reached a manageable stage, the "real" substance abuse counseling can begin. The failure to resolve treatment-barrier issues first would be like the cardiac surgeon attempting to do heart surgery without first opening the patient's chest.

While barriers to treatment involvement are being resolved, orientation to the program rules, goals and resources can be accomplished. The expectation of total abstinence will be addressed in the orientation process and in preparing the client to accomplish the state of abstinence. For many alcoholics/drug addicts, getting clean and dry is the most intimidating task to be imagined. Teaching, encouraging, supporting, and persisting in the abstinence goal is the counselor's most trying and important treatment effort. The next most trying effort is giving the client the tools and motivation to stay abstinent.

At the risk of appearing to minimize the challenge of Stage I treatment, a listing of its broad recovery goals is useful in putting parameters on that early treatment effort. The ultimate goal of Stage I treatment is a stable abstinence and an understanding of the necessity to continue on a long-term treatment program at a more intense level. The following listed Stage I goals are by design limited and general. Their execution should reflect the individual life circumstance, personality, and progress of the disease of each client and each counselor's style. Despite the list's seeming simplicity, to accomplish all the goals within an intensive outpatient program (IOP) of 15 to 20 three-hour sessions will not allow time for attempts at doing heavy therapy. Neither is the CD client ready for 'therapy' this early in recovery. At this point it is helpful to remember the KISS principle, "Keep It Simple, Sir."

Stage I Treatment Plan Goals:

Abstinence (All psychoactive drugs)

Commitment to Treatment Regimen

Learn Own Personal Signs and Symptoms of Addiction

Securing a Drug/Alcohol-Safe Environment

Bonding Involvement With 12-Step Group

Commitment to Personal Recovery Plan

Actively Participate in Treatment Program Process

Learn and Practice Planning Activity/Time-use

Learn How to Make the Most of Treatment

Identify and/or Develop A Personal Support System

Learn to Identify and Avoid Relapse Triggers

Learn the Myths and Facts About Addiction

Learn the Dynamics of Change

Cope With Episodes of Craving/Compulsion

Learn and Understand the Disease of Addiction

Other Mutually Agreed on Goals

Commit to an On-Going Continuing Care Treatment Plan.

The treatment goals are meant to adhere to the broad goals of establishing a stable abstinence, learning the necessity for a long-term recovery program, and the way to get the most from the recovery effort. The goal titles listed above serve the purpose of establishing Stage I level parameters and to provide a logical sequence of addressing the essential knowledge and experiences of early recovery.

There are many possible ways of stating these goals and many measurable objectives to accomplish them. In the appendix a sample treatment plan may be found showing how the Stage I goals may be incorporated in it. The client's approval of the treatment plan is also an agreement to the specific treatment goals and objectives.

Stage I Treatment Homework

The practice of assigning homework activities to clients in the early stage of recovery is frowned upon by some counselors. Others, however, find homework tasks essential to bringing about the necessary changes for recovery. Unless the treatment program is an intensive one, requiring daily attendance, the client may find that the lack of daily supervision, direction and support inadequate to recovery progress. Attention to treatment oriented tasks is recommended six to seven days per week. Such involvement includes attending a self-help group four or more days per week, not counting in-house AA- or NA-type groups. Other activities should include drug and alcohol free leisure-time occupations with family or other support group members.

Homework must not be just busy-work endeavors. They should be carefully chosen to be relevant to goals of positive change. They should be within the capabilities of the client to complete or they will not be accomplished. The completion of the assignments should be expected. Both the client and the counselor must deem them to be important enough that they are reviewed and evaluated at the next counseling session. The client should be taught the value and the skills of planning his own free-time activities that have value in learning or relearning a drug-free life style and drug-free disciplines.

Following is a list of some assignment types, examples of the homework, and how the home-work can be reported in a learning format:

Make alcohol and drug-proof the CD's environment (example, report actions taken to make residence drug and alcohol free).

Safe leisure activities (example, report outcome of a pre-planned leisure activity, a new one or one unused during CD period).

Avoiding trigger people, places, activities and things (example, report a planned and used method of trigger avoidance, such as a new route to work or having a trusted person hold all his cash for him).

Coping with unavoidable trigger situations (example, report what was done specifically to defuse or neutralize what would once have led to a using episode, such as a holiday event or encountering a person formerly associated with heavy alcohol or drug use).

Practicing Serenity Prayer principles (example, report an incident in which the CD person recognized as changeable something he would have previously assumed as being unchangeable).

Practicing the strategies to overcome craving (example, recite from memory 12 means of overcoming or minimizing craving, or report an actual incident in which she successfully used or failed to use strategies to overcome a compulsion to use an addictive substance).

Practice meditation and relaxation exercises (example, report experience, successful or not, of using methods taught as part of Stage I treatment).

Attend and speak-up at AA, NA or CA meetings (example, report her success in achieving this task, and any impact it had on her feelings about the 12-step group or motivation for treatment).

Make planned contacts with a sponsor twice weekly in addition to contacts at 12-step group (example, report the gist of one such conversation).

Read chapters of the Big Book and 12 by 12 (example, discuss with the group or counselor the meaning the reading had for the CD client).

Develop and follow detailed weekend activities schedules (example, learn how and then write activities schedules for the hazardous weekend periods at the end of each week [see Weekend Activities Planning]; report the outcome of the schedule at first session post-weekend).

Tell another support system family member or friend of being in a recovery program. (example: report calling or visiting with a support group member and discussing the CD client's involvement in the recovery program.)

Improve nutrition (example, report on efforts to get on a balanced diet including what was learned from a nutrition lecture).

Enhance physical fitness by walking, running or other exercise five times each week (example, report planned physical fitness program and its level of implementation).

Homework assignments are meaningful only to the extent they enhance, emphasize or accomplish Stage I recovery goals. Unless they are overtly recorded when assigned, and an unwavering requirement that they be reported on and the outcome recorded, their importance will be discounted in the minds of both counselor and client and the program abandoned. Many of recovery's important lessons are learned in the process of putting into practice 'in the field' what was introduced to them via counseling or educational sessions.

How the client adopts and uses out-in-the-world the lessons offered in treatment sessions is probably an accurate reflection of how he will practice them when the treatment has been completed. A light homework program thoughtfully planned and diligently followed is infinitely better than an overly ambitious program that requires more time to carry out than the staff has to devote to it. It is proposed that pertinent homework has the potential of producing such valuable returns that the concept should be used to the limits of the staff's time and the clients' ability to do the assignments.

The counselor's awareness of each of his client's coping skills, social skills, resources, and abilities to control the level of tasks assigned is critical. When the client fails to recognize the relevance of the task, she should be helped to understand it or the task should be changed. Homework and planning skills have a joint therapeutic purpose. Used together they will lead to developing skills and the comfort in the use of free time in recovery lifestyle pursuits. Change occurs when both cognition and the new behavior coexist.

Weekend Activities Planning

Weekends are the most difficult time for many early recovering drug and alcohol addicts. Some have learned better than others how to fill weekends productively in ways that are "safe" and that further the recovery process. Research and painful experience have taught that relapses and treatment abortions most often are the result of negative social interactions, emotional conflicts, and environmental pressures.

Spontaneous drug craving is actually at the bottom of the list of relapse causes. A major coping strategy for the recovering client is the planning of activities to minimize the risk of exposure to these high-risk circumstances. Successful planning skills and their consistent use are high-priority tools for the recovering person. Following are suggestions for producing effective Weekend Activity Plans:

A. Treatment group members should share the experiences they have had to (1) identify high-risk situations that should be avoided, and (2) share strategies that have worked in making safe, free or unstructured time.

B. Each person should write out a detailed description of weekend time - a structure that specifies where she will be, whom she will be with, what she will be doing, when she will be doing it, and how she will be protecting herself against using-triggers.

C. Group members can then share their plans, inviting critiques of them and suggestions for strengthening those plans.

D. AA sponsors and stable group members should be requested to act as escorts or companions in activities that are necessary and that may be unsafe for the recovering person alone.

E. On Monday morning the effectiveness of plans and their execution should be processed. Review the outcomes of the planned activities, identify successes, failures and deviations for the purpose of building a data base for improved future planning. The review process should be conducted as a positive learning exercise. Avoid putting a negative spin on instances of a plan's inadequacies or when the plan is ignored entirely.

F. Activities Planning should become a routine habit of the recovering person, not only during periods of formal treatment, but for two to five years afterwards.

G. Activity Plans should include attendance at 12-step meetings, contacts with sponsor, contacts with persons in personal support group network, and at least one drug-safe recreational activity with supporters of his recovery.

An Activities Plan is only as effective as its execution. Successful carrying out of preplanned activities will give validity to program goals, give the person self-confidence and a growing optimism of recovery potential. Of major importance is the role planning will play in breaking patterns of relying upon compulsive choices of time-use. Thoughtful activities planning will do much to avoid feelings of boredom and temptation.

Chapter XI

ON CD TREATMENT GOALS

The CD counselor's problem is to help the person with a chronic illness adjust to a normal way of life, i.e., stop being sick. With the illness of chemical addiction, adjustment involves adopting what heretofore has been antisocial behavior and culturally deviant attitudes in our drug oriented society. This change includes abstinence and, for a significant period of time, the avoidance of exposure to alcohol and other drug use and users. For the huge majority of recovering chemically dependent people (maybe all of them) life-long abstinence is necessary for continued and life-long recovery.

Accepting the chronic condition as a life-long companion, assuming new attitudes toward social customs, modifying behaviors, gaining a more positive acceptance of self, developing new coping skills, and cultivating an accepting and understanding peer group are major objectives for the chemically addicted person's recovery. The prerequisite for getting well is an unflagging desire to replace the false hope of chemicals with something better. It involves discovering that he is 'sick and tired of being sick and tired' and a determination to get well. It involves finding and using inner strengths.

A number of treatment approaches have not worked very well or not at all. To mention a few:

Aversion Therapy

Chemotherapy (for other than detox)

Psychotherapy (as initial CD treatment)

Antabuse (alone)

TLC (alone)

Guilt or permissiveness

Incarceration or other punishment.

What has worked, often in a combination with professional counseling:

Alcoholics Anonymous

Recovery, Inc.

Women for Sobriety

Surrender

Abstinence

The Whole Person Concept of recovery (PMESS)

Dedication to a planned recovery

Joining the human race

Acceptance of self without the '-ic'.

Three things needed to prepare the alcoholic for recovery are:

1. Accept that they have a CD illness

2. Believe that they can recover

3. Take action for the recovery process to begin.

Points to remember from the wisdom of the AA steps:

1. In order to recover you must come to believe that your life has become unmanageable due to use of an addictive substance.

2. Admitting your powerlessness over alcohol is the first step in learning to manage the disease.

3. In order to recover, you must believe you can.

4. Trust in a power beyond yourself (AA? your sponsor? your treatment group? a wise and trusted friend? your religious faith?) opens the door to hope you can recover (and changes egocentricity).

5. In order to recover you must take some action to allow the process to begin.

6. Be willing to accept and use help in the recovery process.

Patterns of Recovery Based Upon the Jellinek Chart

(This entire progression of recovery steps requires years to accomplish. Be patient! First things first!)

1. Honest desire for help (Recognize the ambivalence).

2. Learns alcoholism is an illness.

3. Told addiction can be arrested.

4. Meets former addicts normal and happy.

5. Stops taking alcohol and psychoactive drugs.

6. Assisted in making personal stocktaking.

7. Right thinking begins.

8. Physical overhaul by doctor.

9. Onset of new hope.

10. Start of group therapy.

11. Regular nourishment taken.

12. Diminishing fears of unknown future.

13. Realistic thinking.

14. Return of self-esteem.

15. Natural rest and sleep.

16. Desire to escape leaves.

17. Adjustment to family needs.

18. Family and friends appreciate efforts.

19. New interests develop.

20. New circle of stable friends.

21. Rebirth of ideas.

22. Faces facts with courage.

23. Increase of emotional control.

24. Appreciation of real values.

25. First steps toward economic security.

26. Confidence of employer.

27. Care of personal appearance.

28. Contentment in sobriety.

29. Rationalizations recognized.

30. Group therapy and mutual help continue.

31. Increasing tolerance (of others).

32. Enlightened and interesting ways of life open up with road ahead to higher levels than ever before.

The counselor's role in an organized program may be limited by time and other factors through the progression of Jellinek's step 11 or 12. From this point support and guidance of a self-help group and sponsor will require the person's growth to be responsible for his continuing recovery.

Other Recovery Points to Remember

The disease of alcoholism may have taken away certain parts of the alcoholic's life, but it provides the challenge of building a new and more meaningful way of life. The CD person must learn to trust the treatment process and the treatment staff. He also must commit to doing what is necessary for recovery. Again, recovery is not just being clean and dry, but changing one's life for the better. Recovery results in many changes, of values, of emotional reactions, of behavior, and of outlook to the way things will be better. The recovered person doesn't cross the street to avoid certain people who know him. Nor does he feel paranoid when a policeman looks his way. Sobriety changes many patterns of behavior for the better.

The recovering alcoholic should be aware of state dependent learning and how it may affect the return to previous skills or knowledge. Alcoholics need not be the victims of their biologies or the past. Nor do they need to be tyrannized by anxious visions to come. They can live in the here and now of the reality of each day as it unfolds. The CD person must learn some 'self-commands'. Relax and take it easy! Slow down! Easy does it! Stop thinking about this! This (recovery process) is no big deal! (Wallace, p.55)

Information is curative. Information explaining black-outs, persistent remorse, resentments, indefinable fears, and anxiety, which can lead to feelings of 'going crazy', contributes to the ability to relax. Treatment in a group setting has many advantages, not the least of which is an awareness of the universality of the human experience.

Objectifying Goals and Making Tasks Relevant

CD treatment should reflect what the disease is that is being treated. The goals and objectives of treatment tasks should follow the treatment rationale that promises to provide the most effective and successful outcome. As discussed in The Nature of Chemical Dependence, the disease is triggered in susceptible persons by the use of psychoactive substances. The susceptibility to the disease has no known identity. The only reliable clue to the susceptibility's possible existence is in its heritability. The common approach to most treatment efforts includes the cessation of the use of addictive substances. In addition to abstinence, successful treatment requires addressing the needs of the whole person that were affected by the CD disease.

The 'traditional' method of CD treatment advocated in this book has a major emphasis on achieving and maintaining a life time abstinence due to its chronic nature which makes the person prone to relapse. The method shuns psychotherapy or mental health treatment methods in early treatment. It favors treatment that takes into account the progressiveness of the disease in both onset and recovery. It further recognizes the necessity of involvement in a structured self-help association as a recovery vehicle during early recovery, and as on-going support during long-term recovery.

The whole person concept in CD recovery may be divided into categories: physical needs including detoxification, medical problems and nutrition; behavioral changes as quitting alcohol and other drug use, practicing skills to overcome compulsivity and to cope with craving, changing behaviors to avoid people, places, things and situations related to alcohol and drug use; emotional aspects related to building and using support systems outside the treatment setting; educational deficits in understanding chemical dependence disease and the person's individual diagnostic signs and symptoms; and the supportive and ancillary systems of the community including environment, leisure pursuits, and support system involvement.

The setting of treatment goals serves several purposes. First, goals provide milestones of progress toward attaining a 'clean and dry' life style, i.e., learning and putting in place a recovering pattern of living. Both the client and the counselor profit by the existence of the guideline of goals in staying on the most effective treatment path. The step-by-step accomplishment of goal attainment provides for the client an encouraging series of recovering successes. The goal successes also provide a record of Phase I recovery progress for the counselor and the HMO or other third-party payer. The goal attainment record will serve as a concrete indicator of readiness for promotion to an advanced level of treatment, the need for concentration in weak areas, or justification for referral to a more intense recovery program.

Goals and tasks must not be busy-work. Stage I goals should be limited to the purposes of abstinence, behavioral changes, attitudinal changes, and learning about and accepting the illness. Deviations from these purposes should be strictly and briefly limited to working through problems that are preventing the primary purpose goals from being reached. Stage I CD counseling may be perceived as the most standardized of treatment stages. Stage I is aimed at cessation of drug use and early recovery indoctrination. It should be visualized as the beginning phase of a long-term recovery process.

There are important reasons for the apparent rigidity and tight boundaries recommended of Stage I goals. First, the goals are consistent with the nature of the chemical dependency disease. The changes strived for are in the areas most realistic to bringing about the arrest of the disease - cessation of addictive substance use and changing related behaviors. The first treatment intervention for the suffering CD person will produce the most dramatic and positive (but not necessarily lasting) changes in how the person feels and in his perception of improvement. This early positive change precedes the 'pink cloud' of irrational optimism and its feelings of having the disease under control. What the CD client learns prior to the 'pink cloud' shutting down openness to learn more, may be all the skills he will have should he decide that no further help is needed, a danger at this point.

The Stage I client must be assisted in doing what she must do to achieve abstinence. She also must be taught the reasons for and importance of abstinence as a life-long condition being necessary to maintaining the arrest of the disease. The cynic, the disbeliever, the misinformed, who will not or cannot accept the evidence for the need of life-long abstinence can be given the choice of maintaining total abstinence for a three month treatment period. All other goals rest upon the basis of the CD client remaining clean and sober. Failure to do so is justification for referral to a residential program providing a protective environment. The only other humane option is a discharge with the right to apply for readmission after achievement of abstinence. The period of three months abstinence will allow the resistant client the time and conditioning for adopting a stronger motivation for recovery.

A Stage I goal is an end product or behavioral change that is essential to recovery. Goals are measurable milestones marking the recovery path. Objectives, which are referred to here as tasks, are things that must occur to reach a specific goal. Tasks are to reinforce, teach or put into practice behavior or attitudinal changes identified as treatment goals. Goals that are not relevant to CD recovery should be avoided. Tasks that do not contribute to the attainment of essential recovery goals should not be assigned.

A list of suggested Stage I goals and possible tasks that may be assigned to assist in arriving at the stated goal is to follow. The goals are basically in priority order for most any CD client. The order of the suggested tasks should be set to meet the recovery needs or capabilities of individual clients. Every CD client may not require the same level of concentration on every listed task, and there may be many who will need to complete tasks not listed. The suggested tasks are among the many areas of guidance and instruction used in an intensive outpatient program in the process of aiding its clients in building the necessary skills and strengths for continuing recovery.

It is recommended that all clients be made aware of and agree to the goals intended and their related tasks. One method of accomplishing this is to incorporate the goals and tasks as written parts of a Master Treatment Plan for review with and commitment to by each client. An example of such a plan may be found in the Appendix. As is obvious by their various natures, some tasks are learning situations in the treatment setting, some appropriately and necessarily are homework assignments, and some are deemed done or failed through observation by staff or others. Some task performances are ongoing changes of behavior and some are one-time actions. A number of tasks are relevant to multiple goals. The importance of any given task may be judged by its range of impact on the achievement of all the goals.

Goal: Abstinence From All Psychoactive Drugs.

Tasks: "Quit Day' achieved.

Negative random urine drug screens.

Accept chemical dependence diagnosis.

Work AA steps 1 and 2.

Give up the struggle to make the old way work.

Goal: Practice a Commitment to Treatment.

Tasks: Understand and agree to program rules and schedules.

Make child-care, job, and other arrangements to attend.

Practice the rules of confidentiality.

Practice openness and honesty.

Overcome urges/temptations to leave or shortcut treatment.

Acknowledge and demonstrate need of help from others.

Interact seriously with other members and staff.

Recognize and accept addiction diagnosis.

Carry out homework assignments.

Goal: Establish a Drug-safe Environment.

Tasks: Live in a drug-free residence.

Work in a drug-free workplace.

Find and use drug-free places of leisure.

Dispose of drug paraphernalia.

Dispose of drug-related telephone numbers.

Move if necessary to accomplish above tasks.

Sever alcohol and drug using and dealing relationships.

Change telephone number if needed to accomplish tasks.

Avoid drug/alcohol using places, activities and people.

Goal: Initiate a Bonding Relationship with a 12-Step Group.

Tasks: Document attendance at 4 or more AA/NA/CA groups weekly.

Strive for 90 meetings in 90 days.

Seek same-sex sponsor with solid sobriety.

Secure one or more 12-step group sponsors.

Participate actively in 12-step group meetings.

Visit other 12-step groups.

Goal: Learn and Practice Activity and Time-use Planning.

Tasks: Write and share with group an action plan for recovery.

Write a plan daily for staying clean and dry today

Develop in writing a safe time-use plan for each weekend.

Keep journal of events where compulsive action was halted.

Share three ways to personally conquer boredom.

Goal: Identify Your 'Triggers' to Drug or Alcohol Use Craving.

Tasks: Share with group your personal triggers to using.

Share with group actions to guard against your triggers.

Plan and practice avoiding avoidable triggers.

Recognize and cope with unavoidable triggers.

Goal: Identify and/or develop a Sobriety Support System.

Tasks: Complete a "Supporters and Underminers" form.

Announce treatment involvement to family, friends, others.

Sever relationships with Underminers.

Bring significant others to 'Open House' session

Get family/significant others in family treatment sessions. Contact daily at least one sobriety support system person.

Goal: Know Myths and Facts about the Addictive Disease.

Tasks: Recognize and share own misconceptions about addiction.

Recognize and share own denial defense patterns.

Recognize and own personal CD signs and symptoms. Know social and behavioral consequences of CD.

Goal: Practice Skills to Cope with Episodes of Craving.

Tasks: Know and use 3 ways to stop craving. (Debate, Distract, Deep-breathe).

Know and use relaxation exercises.

Know and use HALT relapse prevention. (Avoid Hunger, Anger, Loneliness, Tiredness)

Know and use HEDS methods to combat craving. (Get Help, Escape situation; Do something; Slow down).

Know and use 12 more ways to counter craving.

Understand protracted withdrawal.

Write a 'fire plan' of action for craving episodes.

Goal: Understand and Explain CD Disease Processes.

Tasks: Know biopsychosocial nature of CD.

Know general biological/neurological processes of CD.

Learn susceptibilities to CD.

Learn similarities of CD to other chronic diseases.

Learn biopsychosocial costs of CD.

Learn the progressive nature of CD onset and recovery.

Goal: Overcome Compulsion-Directed Behavior.

Tasks: Make plans to resolve financial problems.

Make plans to correct educational deficits.

Make plans to correct occupational deficits.

Stay in here-and-now, not in past or future.

Find safe behavioral substitute for chemical high.

Find safe substitute for chemical escape.

Learn patience - first things first.

Be flexible, adaptable - a survivor.

Find satisfaction in nurturing others.

Be responsible for own recovery.

Goal: Expect a Better Life in Recovering from CD.

Tasks: Avoid self-criticism. Practice positive self-acceptance.

Allow self to grieve for life's unresolved loses.

Give and accept forgiveness.

Accept the nurturing of staff and others.

Be responsible for own behavior, feelings and problems.

There are some fundamental premises necessary to setting effective treatment goals. "Recovery: A return to normal functioning based on total continuous abstinence from alcohol and substitute drugs, corrective nutrition, and an accurate understanding of the disease. The word 'cure' should not be used because it implies that the alcoholic can engage in normal drinking after his 'problem' has been corrected" (Milam and Ketcham, pp. 189). A recovered chemically dependent person is one who maintains total abstinence from psychoactive drugs and has returned to a normal way of life. Being recovered does not mean that the person has become problem free.

Authentic CD treatment does not set goals that imply mental illness or that is moralistic. There does not exist the ex-alcoholic or ex-addict, as such terms imply that a cure has occurred. The CD person must be relieved of the idea that chemical dependence is the result of a character flaw or other psychological inadequacies. The CD disease deserves to be treated as a primary one, not as a symptom of something else. The long-term effects of chemical toxicity, malnutrition, hypoglycemia, cell damage, and withdrawal symptoms have aggravated any psychological problems the person may have.

The existence of a psychological problem may be mistaken as evidence that the CD person is an inadequate, depressed, anxious, and self-destructive personality. This view of the CD's character and personality reinforces the belief that she is responsible for the disease, increases guilt and shame, intensifies anxiety and resentments, and stiffens defensiveness against both diagnosis and treatment.

The CD is responsible for doing what is necessary to get well, and is responsible for chemically affected behavior. The view that psychological or personality problems are the cause of the chemical dependency (i.e., CD being a symptom of a primary psychological problem) will result in a treatment focused upon treating the depression, anxiety, traits of personality, or other presumed psychological dysfunctions rather than the primary disease, chemical dependence. The understanding of CD as a physical disease, the cessation of substance use, and the treatment of medical and nutritional consequences are fundamental in providing the CD person the mental state and physical resources necessary to achieving a quality recovery.

While psychological factors do not cause the disease of chemical dependence, the disease can and frequently does create psychological and emotional problems. Stage I of treatment should not discount the health and behavior change issues by allowing the treatment focus to come to rest on psychological issues that may resolve spontaneously with abstinence and behavior changes.

Chapter XII

The Power of Listening and Other Counseling Skills

The basic principles and techniques of counseling are exactly the same whether we are working with a person with a problem with chemicals or with a person having a problem in any of the many areas of emotional or mental health requiring some manner of change in its resolution. The difference that we must identify is not with the style, technique, or principles of counseling but in the counselor himself.

It is imperative that the counselor of substance abuse clients be deeply knowledgeable about the illness. Unless he is very knowledgeable, several things are likely to occur. First, there may be the setting of treatment goals and objectives that will not result in the client's recovery from his addiction or dependency. Second, the person may be misdiagnosed and the issue of the alcoholism or other drug addiction may not be dealt with in a direct manner. Third, since the multifaceted nature of chemical dependence dictates its treatment strategy, and unless the counselor knows the illness and all its ramifications, she may at best fail to correctly educate the client, or worse, to educate him with invalid information. Fourth, if, or more likely when, the addicted person senses that the counselor knows less about the illness than he, the client, or realizes that the counselor is naive and can be conned, the potential therapeutic relationship will fail to occur or be greatly flawed.

Gilbert Anthony, a much sought after CD counselor of some years ago, said that the foremost attribute of an effective CD counselor is the ability to listen and really hear what his clients say to him. Curtis Schofield, a minister and graduate pastoral counselor friend, identified his most satisfying and effective counseling sessions as those in which he talked the least. The words of these two models of counselor effectiveness rank listening and understanding high on the list of counseling skills.

Empathy is the ability to understand another's problems and to identify with them in that regard. Empathy is a feeling state, lending the ability to "walk in the other's shoes." Empathy does not mean to identify with the other so intensely that the empathizer loses her own identity in the process.

Active listening is the intellectual behavior of hearing what the other is actually saying, understanding it, and communicating that understanding back to the speaker. Caring promotes active listening to the feeling level of empathy. The counselor or therapist reaches his highest level of effectiveness when empathizing with his client.

If we listen well enough, our alcohol or drug dependent client will tell us the way to help him get well. Every effective alcohol and drug counselor knows more about addiction than his clients, and it is necessary to establish that fact very early in the counseling relationship to give confidence in the quality of treatment being offered. The mutuality of counselor empathy and the client's confidence enhances the client's treatment readiness and produces a therapeutic climate.

There are three unhelpful types of counseling:

The counselor who tries to help by rescuing feels superior, gives excessively, has all the answers, wants to run the whole show, is 'top dog' in the relationship, takes responsibility for, smothers, and is permissive.

The persecutor counselor is judgmental, punitive, hostile, vengeful, uncaring, faultfinding, and harshly confrontive.

The victim counselor believes his clients intend to take advantage of him by making him look bad. He is dependent, helpless, feels inferior, is self-discounting, has a poor self-image, and secretly feels he is a loser. He is defensive and takes criticism personally.

The empathic counselor is a helpful counselor and values both her client and herself. She is professionally knowledgeable, a good listener, and a good communicater. She knows her limitations as well as her strengths and applies that knowledge in ways to be of greatest help to her clients. She can and does engage in self- examination and makes opportunities to grow in her professional competence. Her work is client centered.

Quite often the "teaching" counselor clothes his wisdom in self-disclosure, forgetting that the client has probably heard it all before anyway. Counselor self-disclosure, along with other forms of preaching, signals a shutdown of the client's reception of it. However, the client probably may not object because if the counselor is talking the client won't have to. The client is there because of his problem and really isn't receptive to hearing the counselor's recovery experience. Counseling lore tells us that to be effective the counselor must let the client know how well qualified he is in the treating of the addictive disorders. This may be a thankless task. If the client is committed to his own recovery he may view the counselor's efforts to justify his leadership as taking away from attention to the client's problem and focusing attention onto the counselor.

Rapport with the client is more likely gained by listening than by talking. Technique, method or strategy of treatment is less important than being able and willing to listen. The client wants to feel that he or she is really being heard and understood. Therein lies a paradox. The alcohol or drug client, along with a probable majority of the non-addicted public, is full of myths and misinformation about addictive substances, addiction, and what may be required for its recovery. If one follows the method of getting the client to talk while the counselor primarily listens, how is the client to be reeducated?

It is difficult, if not impossible, to be the most effective counselor while at the same time attempting to fill the role of teacher. One solution to the dilemma is to separate the tasks. When other staff are available to provide education specifically, the clients are better able to adapt to the different goals intended, and the counselor can concentrate on the issues of motivation, change and resistance. When other staff are not available to provide separate education and counseling sessions, the individual or group counseling sessions may be planned to divide some are all the sessions between the two tasks. For example, the first part of a session may be designated for counseling issues and the final part of the session reserved for educational matters. The educational session or period should be marked by distribution of study materials and the use of a lecture format.

Client centered counseling, as opposed to counselor centered or authority focused, is believed most effective. These three types of counseling were perceived by Benjamin (1981). He defined client centered counseling as: placing the client central in the interview; the client being responsible for self; the client having authority for self; the client having the capacity to learn and to decide; the client being treated as an equal by the counselor; and the client's own frame of reference and his own subjective view of the world subject to the client's own understanding.

The client centered counselor's responses and leads include silence, eye contact, sounds or body language signifying that the client is being heard, restatements, asking for clarification, reflection of feelings, and some questioning that encourages the client to continue talking and to move the dialogue to a greater depth.

There are numerous ways for questions to be asked. Following are some of those question types, some of their uses, and when they perhaps should or shouldn't be used.

The question is a basic and necessary tool of the counselor, but their use should not be his main role.

Questioning is a subtle teaching tool. When an interview is conducted on an, "I ask; you answer" basis, the client learns to not talk until the counselor asks. The client thus inhibited will say little spontaneously, having decided he should give the counselor what he seems to want. Bombarding the client with questions can be perceived by the client as a weapon wielded against him. The 'prosecuting attorney' will neither establish rapport with a client nor will he communicate caring. A skill of enquiring without seeming to will avoid evoking the client's defensiveness and won't teach him to be silent until questioned.

Indirect questions can be more open to uninhibited responses than will direct questions. "Tell me what happened that makes you seem so sad today." Rather than, "What caused you to be so sad today?" Or, "Andrew, I wonder if you are getting the support you want from your family." Rather than, "Is your family supportive enough for you?" Try, "It must have been tough attending your first AA meetings this week." Rather than, "How did you feel at the AA meetings this week?"

Using the direct form of question is not always avoidable. Such questions may be either open or closed. The closed question is narrow and invites a brief, even a one word, answer. Unless seeking some specific information, such as "Do you have a home telephone?" the closed form of direct question has limited use. In contrast, the open question is broad and invites a wide, detailed or expansive response. Some examples of closed and open ended questions are:

closed: "What's the matter with you today?"

open: "You don't seem yourself today. Has something happened?"

closed: "Did you write down your weekend activity schedule?"

open: "Bill, how do you plan to make your weekend safe?"

Some questions are formed so that the answer is implied, that is, the question includes the answer. If the purpose of such a question is to reinforce a bit of necessary client knowledge, it may be useful.

"Shouldn't you stay away from your brother since you know he is still using?

Such questions that include answers can imply the need to agree with the questioner. That is, the questioner is asking to be agreed with. Questions embedded with a deceitful purpose have questionable value.

"When you visited your brother, knowing he was using, how did you reconcile that to your treatment commitment?"

In a family session, the client angrily asked his wife, "How do you want me to be? What do you want me to do?"

Since the questioner already knew the answers to his questions, the counselor aborted the question and asked the wife not to answer. Confronted, the client agreed that he already knew what she wanted him to be and to do – quit drinking and be a responsible father and husband. The questioner's motive was to force the wife to appear contentious and uncooperative, and he as henpecked – a reason he drank.

Both counselors and clients are able to ask questions to which the answer is already known. Such questions usually have a hidden motive and are often manipulative. Clients' questions to the counselor should be examined closely before answering or not answering. Questions asking for confidential information should not be answered. Questions that are tangential to the topics under discussion can result in losing the purpose or goal of the session, or in taking the focus off a therapeutic interchange. The motive behind such questions may be challenged and the discussion returned to the intended track.

Legitimate client questions seeking information not relevant to the current discussion may be deferred. Questions sometimes provide the client a way of expressing himself. Questions asked to avoid making a self-asserting statement should be challenged by asking the questioner to change her question into a statement. Questions of all kinds challenge the counselor to practice the most used of counseling skills: choosing the response or reaction that is most therapeutic to the client.

Cop-Out Words

Clients in counseling will often use cop-out words, words that signal an unvoiced resistance to change. These words may be used when the client is self-disclosing, describing relationships, or while stating a commitment to a recovery goal. When this form of CD behavior is used, the words actually mean, "I don't really intend to do what I say I want to do," or, "I will not take responsibility for what goes on in my life." Some of the cop-out words are:

because

but

if

can't

except

may

should

try

why

won't

work on it.

The Gestalt therapist calls the use of these words the 'holding-on-bite.' When we use the holding-on-bite we can't chew; we can't swallow, and we can't spit it out. We're stuck with "it."

The client's use of these words must be challenged, when appropriate, to determine exactly what she means. No meaningful treatment goal contract or commitment will contain them. A contract containing cop-out words will be unclear as to real intent and responsibility will surely be sabotaged.

The Portrait of the Ideal CD Counselor

She asks for what she wants -straight. She can say "No" – straight.

She likes people – nonjudgmentally.

She is aware of herself, of any game playing, hidden agendas, any manipulative tendencies, her own feelings, her own 'garbage.'

She is capable of being aware of the other.

She knows that it takes two to play psychological games. She is responsible for herself – for her own feelings – for caring and concern for others.

She is responsible for being honest and open with herself and others.

She does not take responsibility for others' feelings, but is responsive toward feelings of others.

She won't be responsible for others' uninvited expectations of her.

She is responsible for her own realistic expectations of herself.

She is responsible for sharing herself – for giving and receiving – for personal growth and for her life goals and meanings.

The 12 Steps in Understanding Alcoholics

Step 1: I admitted that I was powerless over alcoholics and could not forcibly help them.

Step 2: Came to believe that a power equal to myself lay hidden in the alcoholic and aligned myself with it.

Step 3: Made a decision to have these two powers join hands and practice cooperation as I understood it.

Step 4: To better understand the individual alcoholic, I made a humble and fearless search into his needs, feelings and fears, as well as my own.

Step 5: I constantly urged the alcoholic to be open and share himself with others, with all the dignity and humility befitting a human being.

Step 6: I resolved to always share with the alcoholic my findings about himself, to the maximum extent that his arro- gance and self-criticism would allow doing so con- structively. Step 7: I resolved to be ready to share his pain with him without succumbing to it nor feeling pity for him nor extending special favors because of it.

Step 8: Continued urging him to be human, and to be open and share himself with others.

Step 9: Resolved to be open myself and whenever wrong to readily admit my mistakes -never allowing myself to forget that my power alone cannot keep the alcoholic sober.

Step 10: Continued to take my personal inventory and whenever possible shared my feelings with the alcoholic.

Step 11: Sought through meditation and cogitation, con- sultations and conferences to improve my understanding of the alcoholic and his needs and my ability to help him.

Step 12: Having had a certain understanding and success as the result of these steps, I tried to carry this message to others.

(The foregoing credited to Dr. Alkinoos Vourlekis, and modified.)

Why People Become Clients
Views of Noted Therapists

"Most people become patients because of their un- willingness to accept responsibility for their own lives. In- stead of relying on themselves, most people look to external sources of support." (Frederick Perls, 1969)

"It is the attempt to win the love and approval of others that leads people to give up their internal orientation in deciding on what they value. We learn to distrust what we think, feel, want and believe as we look outside ourselves and adopt standards that we 'should' hold. Clients have lost contact with what they deeply think or feel because they have taken over the conceptions of others as their own... Therapy is largely a process by which clients learn to trust themselves and develop an internal locus of control." (Carl Rogers, 1961, 1969)

"Counselors' lack of success in working with the addictive personality(?) can be attributed to a fundamental inability to understand the 'external' predisposition of the drug-dependent person... People who are described as 'external' are those who tend to place responsibility for their own feelings on someone or something outside themselves. The internally configured individual is giant steps ahead of his externally oriented counterpart, because causality for emotional states is anchored in the self. Internal orientation is seldom a personality configuration which come naturally to those whom it dominates." (Wayne Dyer and John Vriend, 1977)

"Our job is to face this question (the client's morals and values), confront them with their total behavior, and get them to judge the quality of what they are doing. We found that unless they judge their own behavior, they will not change." (William Glasser, 1965)

These well known professionals, and many others, have discovered the significance of the inner-self as the locus of personal strength and responsibility. While Stage I of treatment does not advocate direct assault on morals and values, the effort is centered upon changing behavior and the sense of liability for it. The result is the planting of the seed of thought and action based upon an internal locus of control, decision making and behaviors that are trusting of their own inner strengths.

Dual Disorder

Chemogenic anxiety, mood and behavior disorders have a high rate of spontaneous remission after a period of abstinence from psychoactive drugs and recovery-directed activities. From ten to fourteen days of abstinence should be allowed to expect observable abatement of anxiety and symptoms of depression. Persons who are already being treated with prescribed medications for mental or emotional disorders should be evaluated by a psychiatrist. No decisions regarding medication should be made by a non-physician. Simple depression, anxiety, personality disorders, relationship problems, and most neuroses, even when also chemically dependent, are treatable with drug-free modalities.

Pharmacological methods of treatment should be limited to long-term medications used by persons with dual disorders of thought, mood or behavior that are uncontrollable without medication, and untreatable with psychotherapy alone. These individuals have a high potential for relapse, harm to self or others, or are incapable of functioning independently in society unless medicated.

Special dual disorder treatment programs are becoming more common. The majority of such efforts call upon the resources of both chemical dependence and mental health fields. A high degree of cooperation and coordination is called for in assessment, case management, ancillary services, treatment planning and delivery, and continuing care post treatment of the dual diagnoses client.

"Cliché Therapy"

A concrete, disciplined, simple, and easily grasped counseling approach is needed during the early days, weeks and months of recovery. Most substance abuse counselors know and may also use the principles of what I will call "Cliché Therapy." This title should in no way be taken as a pejorative one. It is meant to give the body of principles incorporated in it the respect it deserves and the recognition of its important role in chemical dependence recovery. Their words of wisdom are useful to the recovering person throughout a lifetime of recovery growth. They are addressed at this point due to their usefulness in providing a set of basic truths that will carry the newly recovering addict through the trauma of early recovery. The name was inspired by a counselor friend, Bill M., who is most creative and effective in the use of adages or maxims in awakening awareness in his clients some needed lesson or insight. A catalog of the most common of these principles follows:

"One day at a time." (Don't drink/use today. Don't live in the past or future – living today is curative).

"First things first." (Getting well is number one).

"Live and let live." (Take care of yourself).

"I am responsible." (No blaming, no scapegoating, no alibiing, no enablers)

"Ninety meetings in ninety days." (Discipline is important).

"One thing at a time." (Patience. Get off the worry racetrack).

"Easy does it." (Slow down. What's the hurry)?

"Everything in its own time." (Overcome compulsive decisions).

"Think - Think - Think!" (Mind over emotions).

"Keep it Simple S....." (KISS) (Don't make recovery complicated).

"But for the Grace of God..." (Practice gratitude and thankfulness).

"God, grant me the Serenity to Accept the things I cannot change, Courage to change the Things I can, and the Wisdom to know the Difference." (Cool it. Accept what is. Being perfect isn't necessary. You can only change yourself).

These timeless guiding principles, slogans, mottoes, clichés, prayers, call them what you will, are traditionally drilled into AA newcomers and promoted by AA-knowledgeable counselors. Many, in a position to make these powerful principles useful tools of early recovery, give them only lip service and then go on to counsel the still befuddled recovery neophyte in areas that are irrelevant to early recovery tasks.

"First things first" means just that. Your client, who has no inkling of what must transpire to achieve recovery and certainly does not know what should be dealt with first, and wants everything fixed at once. Quite mistakenly she wants to mend all her damaged fences at once; she wants to be exorcised of her guilt, her doubts, her impatience, her craving – at once. Fractured relationships and knotty spiritual issues are demanding a quick fix. At the outset she wants to get well now, to feel better without really having to change and without having to listen to what there is to learn about recovering. In a word, the new chemically dependent client wants to "eat the whole cow" at once. Cooler, more experienced heads know that it must be done one bite at a time and by starting at the right end of the process.

The author confesses that years ago he was among those who thought that the AA slogans were valid and worth practicing by the newly recovering person. But (Have you noticed how "buts" often lead us astray?) professional therapeutic skills should take precedence over trite clichés. Right?

No, not at all. But, (There's that word, again.) it seemed so logically illogical that focusing on these recovery principles was appropriate and important for the client, but it was okay for the counselor to focus on the really important therapy instead. The counselor who reacts thus to the client's addictive thinking and feeling may very well leave his client only partially prepared to travel the recovery route with perseverance or to lose her altogether. It has since been proven over and over that we must hear and respond to whatever concerns are expressed by our neophytes and address them in keeping with what must be "first" to maximize recovery potential. Then bring back into focus the principles and the behavioral changes that are needed to achieve a stable recovery.

Learning these principles and making the physical and behavioral changes necessary to separate the client from a high risk environment and a high risk social milieu comprise an effective Stage I recovery. "Cliché therapy" is believed to be the only "therapy" that the befuddled state and addictive thinking patterns of the newly recovering person can comprehend and utilize for a significant period of time. Dr. Joe Pursch (who treated one U.S. president's wife and another's brother of drug and alcohol dependence) declares that psychotherapy is not appropriate treatment until the achievement of one year of sobriety.

The necessity for complete abstinence from alcohol and other drugs demands the position of number one priority among treatment goals. A guiding rule-of-thumb for the CD counselor is to treat Stage I clients exclusively in the issues directly or closely related to achieving and maintaining abstinence. Norman Miller (p. 62) calls attention to the diagnostic criteria of DSM-III-R which indicates that addictive disorders are considered independent from other psychiatric disorders. Dr. Larry Wharton concurs in the limiting of treatment modalities for persons in the first year of sobriety to the business of staying abstinent (personal communication). Staying clean and sober is a more complex task than many believe, certainly beyond the "Why doesn't he just quit?" comments of the problem-of-willpower crowd. Staying alcohol and drug free for the addict depends upon the adoption and management of a new life style and all that entails.

Alcoholics and other drug addicts are particularly subject to the phenomenon of state dependent learning. Learning acquired while in a drug affected mental state may be inaccessible to clearly recall or use while in a non-drugged mental state. The learning itself may be misunderstood or distorted by the mind still foggy from the chemical abuse. Heavy alcohol and drug users have deficiencies in learning, decision-making, and memory for at least a month after use, and for many addicts deterioration has progressed so far that the complete return of the ability to comprehend requires much more time.

Further, dysfunctional levels of mood and/or attention disorder may exist which will interfere with the delivery of psychotherapy intended to lead to chemical dependence recovery. Milam (*Under the Influence*, p.14) states, "Psychotherapy diverts attention from physical causes of the disease, compounds the alcoholic's guilt and shame, and aggravates rather than alleviates his problems." Psychotherapy was born of the need to treat persons non-medically who are suffering with mental and emotional disorders. Offering psychotherapy in treatment of the addictive illness makes the implication that alcoholism or other chemical addictions have a psychological cause. In addition to the questionable premise that the disease should be treated by eliminating the 'cause', the mistake is compounded by the error of concentrating on 'treatment' of its consequences.

A psychiatrist asked a substance abuse counselor to consult with him about a psychiatric patient whom the psychiatrist had been seeing for two or three years and whom he had come to believe was alcoholic. The patient was not making any recovery progress, nor had the doctor succeeded in getting him to stop drinking. On his weekly visits, the patient frequently smelled strongly of liquor and on more than one occasion had arrived obviously intoxicated. For some time, the patient had been unable to function socially or occupationally in keeping with his education and intellect. Alcohol abuse seemed associated with this dysfunction.

"The first thing you must do," the counselor advised the doctor, "is to get him to quit drinking. Otherwise, improvement in any of his problems is unlikely."

"But how can I do that?" the doctor responded. "I've told him repeatedly that he must stop drinking."

"I would try to enlist family members in an intervention to coerce him to quit; tell him he must quit or you would not be his doctor any longer; or, if all else fails, commit him to the state mental hospital," said the counselor.

The doctor wasn't convinced that any of the suggestions were viable options for him with the problem patient. Annually, for three years, the doctor requested consults with the counselor, and each time the question was the same, the advice was the same, and so was the doctor's reaction. And so was the patient's condition.

Two years after the counselor had left the doctor's agency, the two of them met at a retirement party for a mutual friend. "By the way," said the counselor, "what ever happened to Mr. ....? Did he ever get sober?"

"No," the doctor said. "He never stopped. I saw him for some time after you and I talked last, but then he died."

"Oh," exclaimed the counselor. "What did he die of?"

"Cirrhosis of the liver," said the doctor.

Stage I of recovery begins as soon as the person becomes totally abstinent from alcohol and other drugs. It is the beginning of a long process of doing the things, learning the things, and changing the things that will eventually lead to a stable recovery. At that entry point begins the recognition of how much of the person's life has been derailed. To the experienced eye of the chemical dependence counselor the newly abstinent addict presents as a disaster waiting to be salvaged, to be rehabilitated.

Most counselors will have accepted the label of addictions being a disease if not totally embracing the disease theory. The resulting belief or understanding about the nature of the disease will determine how she will decide the direction of the treatment. The counselor will recognize a whole range of problems that need to be addressed. The client himself will be persuasive about which area of his pain is in need of relief, usually emotional, intellectual or relationship. The counselor will be urged to don the role of psychotherapist and comply with the client's wish to have all his problems solved wholesale.

Treating disturbed relationships, mental or emotional pain, mood disorders, or personality problems is, perhaps unwittingly, treating the disease of substance dependence as a psychological or psychiatric disorder. This observation is not to imply that these issues are unimportant, but, first things first. Step I of recovery is not the time for psychotherapy or mental health counseling unless there is a clear cut dual diagnosis. The biopsychosocial-environmental disease of chemical dependence results in many undesirable and abnormal conditions in every area of the person's life.

We know from ample experience that with enough time in an alcohol and drug-free state, the addiction-caused emotional and mental symptoms will spontaneously abate or cease to exist. It may take three to six months post-withdrawal for symptoms of depression, anxiety, anger, and others to abate.

Stage I must be a time of decision making for the addict. It will be a time of confidence and hope building when the addict experiences the rewards of understanding his illness (that he isn't evil or crazy), of building a positive support system, of clearing his environment of risks to his sobriety, of winning battles against relapse triggers, of coping with the physical and mental changes resulting from withdrawal and post-acute withdrawal, and of a growing realization that he is not alone.

What, then, are the "counseling" priorities of the counselor working with clients in Stage I of recovery? The most helpful role may be a multifaceted one of advising, teaching, demonstrating, encouraging, problem solving, role-modeling, and leading. Does this sound like a non-enabling, caring, but strict parent? Stage I calls for such direct, demanding guidelines due to the usual deficient ability of the client to make healthy decisions. Insight-oriented, depth, unmasking, psychoanalytic, or dynamic psychotherapies are ineffective at this stage of recovery. Neither is it the time to heal crippled relationships. Clients should be discouraged also from starting new romantic relationships while in Stage I as they can be hazardous to recovery (Mooney, et al., p. 185).

Milam (p. 151-52) recommends encouraging the client to confront his drinking life style, but cautions the counselor to refrain from any attempts to analyze behavior, uproot past traumas, identify psychological problems, or resolve conscious or unconscious conflicts. He believes that trying to analyze drinking behavior in these terms will heighten guilt, shame, resentments, and frustrations. The more effective alternative is to build up self-confidence and self-respect, and to encourage normal interactions with the staff and other clients.

Issues beyond the struggle for sobriety accompany the newly recovering person into treatment. Relationship, employment, financial, legal, and other problems can be demanding immediate attention. The counselor and other staff must help the client to evaluate the immediacy of the demanding issues. Staff, such as a case manager, and available community resources may be employed in resolving or neutralizing pressing issues, with the counselor having to deal only with those problems which may directly prevent the achievement of abstinence and other Stage I goals. The use of brief cognitive-behavioral interventions in preventing problems from sabotaging sobriety and the completion of Stage I recovery tasks is recommended. Like chemical dependence therapy, cognitive approaches are direct, have behavior-change outcomes, and enlist the total involvement of the client.

The deterioration of the spiritual aspect of a person's life is probably the first victim of the destructiveness of addiction. A broad definition of spirit is referred to as it applies to the use of "cliché therapy". AA's second step is appropriately placed in second priority for the newly recovering person's growth in that it emphasizes a need to abandon the false fronts of arrogance, conceit, self-sufficiency, and omniscience. Failure to do so would leave the recovery seeker closed to the help that may be his salvation. Quite enmeshed in the addict's resistance to being in need of help from others is his self-image and self-esteem. The principles of "cliché therapy" provide for the client an avenue to changing defensive thoughts and egoistic feelings without the damage to his facade that would cause him to flee from treatment. It is not a great stretch to view the use of "cliché therapy" slogans as a first spiritual awakening of a new positive self-perception. A self-perception based on the wisdom of these pithy principles of living can be a great stride toward serenity. The heavier religious aspects of step two can wait until a greater state of stable sobriety when he will be capable of making some lasting decisions regarding his relationship to a supreme being.

Stage I of CD counseling may be summarized thus: Limited to supporting the client in bringing about changes in alcohol and drug use, connecting with and building a personal support system, creating a drug-use safe environment, developing a new drug-safe life style, remaining receptive to learning, having patience and having hope for the future. "Cliché Therapy" can provide guiding principles to under gird all these do-it-yourself treatment goals. How long the accomplishment of Stage I will take depends upon a multitude of variables - the validity and strength of motivation, and the state of advancement of the disease, among others.

First things for the newly recovering client are learning and practicing the thoughts and behaviors that are consistent with a drug and alcohol free life style.

Appendix

Phases of CD Recovery/Treatment - An Outline   170

Drug-Use History: Assessment of Acute Withdrawal Potential (Form)   172

Progressive Stages of Alcohol Withdrawal   174

Anticipating Potential Severity of Alcohol Withdrawal Complications (Table)   175

Psychoactive Substance Dependence: DSM IV Criteria (Form)   176

Assessment of CD Using Public Health Disease Model   177

Some Signs and Symptoms of Chemical Dependence/ Addiction   178

Eligibility Questionnaire: Criteria for Admission Readiness (Form)   179

Psychosocial Assessment (Form)   181

Mental/Emotional Health Impression (Form)   186

How Severe is My Addiction? (form)   190

Taking A Look at Your Support System (Form)   192

Meeting Attendance Record (Form)   193

Master Treatment Plan (Form)   194

Continuing Care Planning   196

Master Treatment Plan Processes (Form)   198

Three Ways to Stop Craving; Debate, Distract, Deep-Breathe   202

Stage I Treatment Summary   205

A Progressive Recovery Tour Guide   208

PHASES OF CD RECOVERY/TREATMENT

PHASE I LIFESTYLE STRUCTURING: 1 to 3 months

Abstinence from psychoactive drugs

(Detox prn; withdraw from nonessential Rx medications; carry out Quit Day procedure prn; produce random negative UDSs.)

Environmental changes

(Establish a drug-free residence, a drug-safe workplace and drug-free leisure-time places.)

Behavioral changes

(Tell family & friends about your treatment; sever relations with all drug users and sellers; identify and use trigger-free routes to shop, work or play; withdraw from potentially emotion-disruptive relations; say "NO" to invitations to use in words and actions; consciously build and learn to use a personal support system; bond to 12-step self-help group by frequent attendance and involvement; get a sponsor; plan specific drug-free recreation and other leisure and social activities.)

Cognitive changes

(Accept having an addictive illness; learn and remember positive benefits of recovery; learn and practice HALT and HEDS; learn and understand the disease concept of addiction; identify and change addictive thinking; learn and identify with powerlessness and unmanageability language of Step 1 of AA/NA.)

Affective changes

(Bond with treatment group members; ask for support & give support; learn the addict's "land mines" in society's "mine-field"; learn avoidable and unavoidable triggers and fear them; learn about relapse and its danger signs; emotionally experience the hope of recovery; postpone any major life decisions except to recover from addiction; put staying clean and sober life's first priority.)

II SOLIDIFYING RECOVERY: 9 months to 2 years

Continue and strengthen the lifestyle restructuring tasks of phase one

(Strengthen bond with non-drug using culture; expand personal support network and practice using it; individualize personal issues at a low intensity [KISS]; postpone major relationship changes; postpone psychological issues such as "uncovering" or emotional/mental conflicts unless specifically endangering sobriety now; learn and practice relapse prevention skills; resolve physical and health issues; maintain high level of involvement in treatment activities; learn and practice good problem solving skills; make constant use of time-structure planning to minimize risk of exposure to unsafe situations; practice avoidance of triggers; practice recognition of positive recovery gains by self and others.)

III INDIVIDUALIZING RECOVERY: 2 to 4 years

Persevere in continuing to follow previously learned recovery practices

(Maintain close ties with drug-free culture and personal support groups; abstinence; expand necessary exposure to non-recovering community with caution and be prepared to cease any contacts which threaten recovery; reestablish damaged relationships; make amends; repair any career or job damages; get needed psychological and relationship therapy/counseling; focus on spiritual growth.)

IV MAINTAINING RECOVERY: for life

Lifelong abstinence from psychoactive drugs, ongoing attention to healthful living and healthy relationships. Maintain contacts with 12-step mutual help group. Extended involvement is recommended.

© S. Ed Hale, 7/10/99 Copyright reserved.

DRUG-USE HISTORY

ASSESSMENT OF ACUTE WITHDRAWAL POTENTIAL
(Page 1 of 2)

Date _____ Time _____

Name _____ SS # ____ - ___ - _____

PART A:

1. What was the time and quantity of last used:

   Alcohol (what form?): _____

   _____

   Other drugs (include prescribed and proprietary drugs):

   _____ _____ _____

   _____ _____ _____

2. How much alcohol and other drugs were used in past
   24 hours _____

   _____

   Used in past week _____

   _____

3. Last 24 hour period of drug and alcohol abstinence

   _____

   Explain_____

   Any withdrawal symptoms*_____

4. Have you ever received medical care for alcohol or
   drug use? _____ When _____
   Where_____
   Give details_____

   _____

5. Have you ever had seizures? _____ Describe _____

   _____

6. Have you ever had hallucinations?_____ Describe_____

   _____

7. Describe presenting condition:
   Asymptomatic (sober)__ Intoxicated: Mild___ Moderate___ Severe____
   Acute Abstinence Syndrome stage_____. Describe
   symptoms* _____

   _____

   *Be specific. Avoid generalities such as "DTs" or "sick".

8. Vital signs: Pulse_____ BP_____ Temp._____ Resp._____.

(Page 1 of 2) Complete Part A at time of admission!

Assessment of Withdrawal Potential
(Page 2 of 2))

PART B:

The preceding questions (PART A) are pertinent to evaluating the Acute Abstinence Syndrome. Withdrawal Stages 2, 3 or 4 (in question 7) should be reported at once to the physician on duty. The following questions (PART B) are pertinent to evaluating the chronicity of the chemical dependence. Postpone PART B if medical treatment to abort progression to severe stages of withdrawal is needed.

9. Describe the pattern of your drug-alcohol use _____
_____
_____

10. Have you ever experienced blackouts? _____
    Describe_____
    _____

11. Are you allergic to any food or drug?_____
    What?_____

12. Age at first alcohol use _____

13. Age at first other drug use _____ What drug?
    _____

14. Age at beginning of regular alcohol use _____

15. Age at beginning of regular drug use _____ What
    drugs? _____
    _____

16. Year of first problem use _____

17. Have you ever received psychiatric, psychological or counseling treatment because of alcohol or other drug use? _____ When? _____
    Where? _____
    Give details _____
    _____
    _____

18. Name of person validating this information _____
    Relationship to client _____

History taken by:_____
Action taken: _____
_____
_____

THE PROGRESSIVE STAGES OF THE ALCOHOL WITHDRAWAL SYNDROME

Symptoms - Some or All of the Following

Stage 1. Psychomotor agitation

Autonomic hyperactivity

(tachycardia

hypertension

hyperhydrosis)

Anorexia

Insomnia

Illusions

Stage 2. Some or all of Stage 1 symptoms, plus:

Hallucinations

Stage 3. Some or all of Stage 1 and 2 symptoms, plus:

Disorientation

Delusions

Delirium

Stage 4. Seizure activity in addition to Stage 3 symptoms.

Seizure activity may precede or complicate any of the above stages. Rule out other possible causes of seizure.

When a patient reaches stage 3, he may be expected to have other complications, such as infection, trauma, multiple-drug abuse, hypovolemia, severe fluid and electrolyte disturbances, and/or pancreatitis. Get medical consultation!

ANTICIPATING POTENTIAL SEVERITY OF ALCOHOL WITHDRAWAL COMPLICATIONS

A means of anticipating the ultimate severity of alcohol withdrawal syndrome is based upon determining the quantity of alcohol consumed and the duration of the drinking episode. The relation of the daily drinking pattern to the severity of alcohol withdrawal complications was offered by Dr. Robert B. Johnson in the old Quarterly Journal of Alcoholism. At the time of his article the high possibility of the alcohol user also concurrently using other drugs was not a concern and was not taken into account in his article "Alcohol Withdrawal Syndromes". Despite that omission, the following table of relationships can be a helpful reference to the clinician concerned with aborting the potential escalation of withdrawal complications via medication.

Amt. consumed daily	Duration in days	Withdrawal symptoms
1 pint of whiskey, or	2 to 10	Tremors
1 quart of wine, or	11 to 21	Hallucinations
5 quarts (14 cans) of beer	22 or more	Delirium tremens
1 fifth of whiskey or	2 to 3	Tremors
2 quarts of wine, or	4 to 7	Hallucinations
8 quarts (1 case) of beer	10 or more	Delirium tremens

PSYCHOACTIVE SUBSTANCE DEPENDENCE
DSM IV CRITERIA ASSESSMENT QUESTIONNAIRE

Customer's Name _____

Specify the substance(s) being used/abused: _____ Three or more of the following occurring in same 12-month period.

1. Do you find that it takes up to one and a half times as much of the substance to intoxicate or to give the desired effect as it did the first time you used it?   yes____   no____
Or does it take less than it used to? yes____   no____

2. Have you experienced withdrawal symptoms that are characteristic of the substance you have been using?   yes____   no____   If "yes", describe the symptoms: _____
Have you ever taken the same or similar substance to relieve or avoid withdrawal symptoms?   yes____   no____

3. Have you ever used(or drunk) more than you intended or used (drunk) for a longer period than you intended? yes____   no____

4. Do you have a persistent desire or made unsuccessful efforts to cut down or to control your substance use?   yes____   no____

5. Do you spend a great deal of time in getting, using, or recovering from the effects of psychoactive drugs?   yes____   no____

6. Has substance use or its effects resulted in your giving up or reducing important social, occupational, or recreational activities? yes__no__
Or has such use interfered with obligations at home, work, or school? yes____   no____
Or have you engaged in physically hazardous activity (e.g., driving or operating machinery) when under the influence of the substance? yes____   no____

7. Have you continued the substance use despite a persistent or recurrent social, psychological, or physical problem that is caused or exacerbated by use of the substance?   yes____   no____

Specify if: **With Physiological Dependence** (Crit.1 or 2 present) ___
– or –
Without Physiological Dependence (neither 1 nor 2 present) ___

Diagnosis _____

Assessor Signature and Credentials _____

ASSESSMENT OF CD USING PUBLIC HEALTH DISEASE MODEL

A. SUSCEPTIBLE HOST
(Often undetected or undetectable prior to onset of the disease.)
Pre-illness susceptibility indicators:
Rampant CD family history
High 'natural' tolerance
Experiences high level of subjective positive effects from
  substance use
Use as self-medication
Heavy or frequent 'recreational' use
External locus of control
Unresolved life stressors.
(CONFIRMED SUSCEPTIBILITY INDICATES SUBSTANCE-
USE RELATED ANOMALIES OF BRAIN CHEMISTRY AND/
OR METABOLISM).

PLUS+ B. ADDICTIVE SUBSTANCE
Alcohol
Psychotropic medications (both prescribed and OTC)
  Illegal drugs
Addictive non-food or non-beverage substances, e.g., OTC
  remedies, volatile hydrocarbons.

PLUS+ C. A COMPATIBLE/CONDUCIVE ENVIRON-MENT
Easy availability of addictive substance
Alcohol or drug using associates
Social setting accepting of substance use
Social setting tolerant of substance abuse
Leisure activities that involve substance use.

EQUALS = THE DISEASE OF CHEMICAL DEPEN-DENCE OR ADDICTION

SOME SIGNS AND SYMPTOMS OF CHEMICAL DEPENDENCE/ADDICTION

Physical tolerance to substance effects

Withdrawal symptoms when abstinent

Taking alcohol or other psychoactive substance to relieve or avoid withdrawal symptoms

Episodes of:

Using more of the substance than intended

Using for longer periods than intended

Using at inappropriate times or places (e.g., at work, driving or operating dangerous equipment, etc.)

A persistent desire to cut down or control use

Unsuccessful efforts to quit, cut down, or control use

Use has resulted in giving up or reducing important social, occupational, or recreational activities

Used while engaged in physically hazardous activities

Use has interfered with obligations at home, work, or school

Continued use despite a persistent or recurrent social, psychological or physical problem caused or exacerbated by use of substance

Denial of evidence of the disease state, e.g., minimizing, alibiing, blaming, rationalizing, avoiding, etc.

Anxiety attacks at prospect of ceasing use or inaccessibility of drug of choice

Choosing associates who use and activities where alcohol or addictive substances are typically used

Using surreptitiously

Protecting and assuring availability of supply

Disruption of relationships due to substance related behaviors

Recurring legal infractions or accidents

Concern expressed by family or close friends over substance use and related behaviors.

ELIGIBILITY QUESTIONNAIRE
CRITERIA FOR ADMISSION READINESS

Answers to this questionnaire will help to determine whether the substance abuse intensive outpatient program is appropriate for the applicant. Applicants not meeting the program's criteria should be referred to a more suitable treatment.

1. Yes No (circle one): I am available to attend the program regularly for five to seven weeks.

2. Yes No :I have or can arrange the transportation needed.

3. Yes No :Work, child care, or other duties will not interfere with my keeping the stated program schedule.

4. Yes No :I will commit to also attend at least four AA meetings per week for a minimum of 6 months.

5. Yes No :I accept the program staff's diagnosis that meets the DSM IV criteria for substance dependence.

6. Yes No :I am 18 years old or older.

7. Yes No :I am willing to commit to abstinence from all controlled substances and alcohol for the entire period of treatment.

8. Yes No :I have no pending legal cases that could result in incarceration and thus interrupt treatment.

9. Yes No :I do not intend to move from the area for at least one year.

10. Yes No :I am willing to postpone any vacation until after the completion of treatment.

11. Yes No :I have a source of income that does not include the trafficking or handling of drugs in any way.

12. Yes No :I have one or more drug-free family members or close friends who are willing and able to be involved in the family portion of my treatment.

13. Yes No :I have a case manager of a local social service or mental health agency who will assist and monitor my community stabilization activities (e.g., housing, job training, education, financial assistance, etc.)

Case Mgr. sig._____

Agency_____

Applicant sig._____

Date_____

PSYCHOSOCIAL ASSESSMENT

Name _____

Address _____

_____Phone_____

Birthplace_____

DOB_____ Age_____

PRESENTING PROBLEM _____

_____

PRECIPITATING EVENT _____

_____

WORK HX & STATUS_____

_____

_____

_____

LEGAL HX (DUIs, arrests, charges pending, convictions, probation/parole)

_____

_____

_____

_____

_____

PHYSICAL HEALTH HX & STATUS_____

_____

_____

_____

Psychotropic Meds & Dosages _____

_____

_____

Prescribing Physician_____

OTC Meds _____

Allergies _____

MENTAL HEALTH HX & STATUS_____

_____

_____

_____

_____

Suicidal?_____ Homicidal?_____

If Yes to either, describe response _____

_____

SUBSTANCE ABUSE HX & STATUS (all being used, age
at 1st use, treatments)_____

_____

_____

_____

_____

FAMILY:

Father:_____

Living?_____ A&D Prob?_____

Occupation _____

Relationship with Client_____

Mother:_____

Living?_____ A&D Prob?_____

Occupation_____

Relationship with Client_____

Parents' Marital Relationship (sep., divorced, deceased, widowed, etc.)_____

Siblings (List by name, sex, age, relationship, A&D problems if any)

_____

_____

_____

_____

_____

Client's Birth Order_____

A&D PROBLEMS IN THE FAMILY (Aunts, Uncles, Grandparents)_____

_____

EMOTIONAL/MENTAL PROBLEMS IN FAMILY_____

_____

_____

_____

CLIENT'S DEVELOPMENTAL HX _____

_____

_____

_____

_____

CLIENT'S MARITAL HX & STATUS_____

_____

_____

Reasons for any Separations or Divorces_____

_____

_____

Name of Spouse/Companion_____

Address if different:_____

_____

Employment:_____

Does Spouse/Companion use alcohol or drugs? _____

Does Spouse/Companion have A&D problem? _____

Does Spouse/Companion have Emotional/Mental problem?

_____

CHILDREN (List by name, sex, age, & if in Client's custody or not)_____

_____

_____

_____

_____

CHILD or PARENTING PROBLEMS? _____

_____

_____

_____

_____

_____

Children at home not in school? _____

_____

Is Child Care needed when you are absent from home?____

EDUCATION (Highest grade client completed & any Specialty Training)_____

CURRENT HOME & ENVIRONMENT (Description and qualitative evaluation)_____

_____

_____

_____

_____

_____

ESTIMATED CURRENT LEVEL OF FUNCTIONING (Rate: Good, Fair or Poor)

Work_____ Parenting_____ Marital_____

Social_____ Mental_____ Emotional_____

Behavioral_____ Physical_____

STAFF COMMENTS:_____

_____

_____

_____

_____

_____

_____

Staff Signature & Credentials_____

_____ Date _____

MENTAL/EMOTIONAL HEALTH IMPRESSION

Name_____

Date_____

APPEARANCE
( )Appropriate
( )Unusual
( )Meticulous
( )Unkempt
( )Disheveled
( )Bizarre

HYGIENE
( )Appropriate
( )Inappropriate

MOTOR BEHAVIOR
ACTIVITY LEVEL
( )Normal
( )Fidgety
( )Overactive
( )Agitated
( )Overly controlled
( )Mildly retarded
( )Lethargic
( )Unsteady

ATTITUDE
( )Compliant
( )Cooperative
( )Hopeful
( )Optimistic
( )Distrustful
( )Suspicious
( )Aggressive
( )Hostile
( )Uncooperative
( )Demanding
( )Panicky
( )Fearful
( )Sarcastic

AFFECT QUALITY
( )Appropriate
( )Flat
( )Exaggerated
( )Labile
( )Bizarre

MENTAL/EMOTIONAL HEALTH IMPRESSION
- page.2 -

MOOD
( )Normal
( )Sad
( )Tearful
( )Detached
( )Angry
( )Resentful
( )Elated
( )Euphoric
( )Grandiose
( )Variable

SPEECH
( )Normal
( )Slow
( )Rapid
( )Pressured
( )Logical
( )Bizarre
( )Detailed
( )Repetitive
( )Precise

STREAM OF THOUGHT
( )Normal
( )Confused
( )Delusional
( )Tangential
( )Circumstantial
( )Obsessional
( )Hallucinations
( )Blocking

ORIENTATION
( )times four
( )times three
( )times two
( )times one
( )not disoriented

JUDGEMENT
( )Above average
( )Normal
( )Impaired
( )Severely impaired

MENTAL/EMOTIONAL HEALTH IMPRESSION

- page.3 -

SUICIDAL IDEATION OR INTENT

( )No ideation or intent

( )Ideation no intent

( )Ideation and intent

HOMICIDAL IDEATION OR INTENT

( )No ideation or intent

( )Ideation no intent

( )Ideation and intent

DEFENSE MECHANISM
Observed as follows

( )Denial

( )Projection

( )Minimizing

( )Intellectualizing

( )Avoidance

( )Blaming

( )Justifying

( )Maximizing

LONG TERM MEMORY

( )Above average

( )Adequate

( )Mildly impaired

( )Severely impaired

SHORT TERM MEMORY

( )Above average

( )Adequate

( )Mildly impaired

( )Moderately impaired

( )Severely impaired

INSIGHT

( )Above average

( )Adequate

( )Fair

( )Poor

( )Very poor

ABSTRACT REASONING

( )Above average

( )Normal

( )Impaired

( )Severely impaired

Assessor's Comments_____

_____

_____

_____

_____

_____

_____

_____

_____

Signature of Assessor_____

Credentials _____

HOW SEVERE IS MY ADDICTION?

Read each question. If the answer to a question is yes, put a check mark on the line next to the number. Each check mark indicates an increased degree of addiction.

___ 1. Do you or those close to you ever worry about your drugging?

___ 2. Are ever unable to stop drugging when you want to?

___ 3. Do you work hard to get your drug? Does it take a lot of time, effort, and planning?

___ 4. Has your drugging ever created problems between you and someone close to you?

___ 5. Have you ever missed work or been late to work because of your drugging?

___ 6. When a time for getting high is approaching, do you think about it often and eagerly look forward to it? Are you extremely disappointed when the expected drug is not available or when it is poor quality? When it is used up?

___ 7. Have you ever neglected your family, your work, or other important obligations because you were drugging?

___ 8. Have you ever been in the hospital or jail because of your drugging?

___ 9. Have you been unable to stop using until all the drug is gone or all the money is gone?

___ 10. Have you given up or reduced important social or recreational activities because of drugging?

___ 11. Have you been unable to enjoy yourself (e.g., at parties) without drugs?

____ 12. Have you continued to drug despite problems such as depression, financial difficulties, or inability to get up in the morning?

____ 13. Have you used in inappropriate places such as work? Are you very protective of and secretive about your supply?

____ 14. Has your use become more frequent or regular?

By Permission: McAuliffe & Albert. (1992). Clean Start. Guilford Press. p. XIX

TAKING A LOOK AT YOUR SUPPORT SYSTEM

Complete carefully the three lists below: Supporters are people who are happy about your efforts to quit drinking and drugging.

Neutrals are those who don't care about your abstinence, one way or the other. Underminers are chemically dependent or abusers themselves, and would prefer that you keep doing the same. You will want to spend a lot of your time with the Supporters, and avoid Underminers entirely!

SUPPORTERS _____

_____

_____

_____

_____

NEUTRALS _____

_____

_____

_____

_____

UNDERMINERS _____

_____

_____

_____

_____

Client Signature _____

MEETING ATTENDANCE RECORD

Name_____

Must attend_____ 12-step meetings per week.

Meeting Place_____

Meeting Date_____

Witness_____

Meeting Place_____

Meeting Date_____

Witness_____

Meeting Place_____

Meeting Date_____

Witness_____

Meeting Place_____

Meeting Date_____

Witness_____

Meeting Place_____

Meeting Date_____

Witness_____

Meeting Place_____

Meeting Date_____

Witness_____

SEH

MASTER TREATMENT PLAN

CLIENT'S NAME:_____

This Date:_____

Admission Date:_____

Projected Discharge Date:_____

DIAGNOSIS: Axis I _____

_____

_____

Axis II _____

_____

_____

Axis III _____

_____

Axis IV _____

_____

_____

Axis V   Present GAF:_____   GAF Year Ago:_____

ASSESSMENT:
STRENGTHS: _____

_____

_____

_____

_____

WEAKNESSES: _____

_____

_____

_____

_____

DISCHARGE CRITERIA (OBJECTIVE):_____

_____

_____

_____

_____

_____

FOLLOW-UP:_____

_____

_____

_____

STAFF SIGNATURE_____

Date _____

MY TREATMENT PLAN HAS BEEN REVIEWED WITH
ME BY A STAFF MEMBER.

CLIENT SIGNATURE _____

Date _____

CONTINUING CARE PLANNING

CLIENT'S NAME_____

MEDICAL:_____

_____

_____

OUTPATIENT SERVICES:_____

_____

_____

_____

VOCATIONAL/EDUCATIONAL NEEDS:_____

_____

_____

_____

REFERRALS MADE TO:_____

_____

_____

_____

_____

FINANCIAL NEEDS: _____

_____

_____

_____

PSYCHOSOCIAL/ENVIRONMENTAL NEEDS:_____

_____

_____

OTHER:_____

_____

_____

STAFF SIGNATURE _____

Date _____

CLIENT SIGNATURE _____

Date _____

MASTER TREATMENT PLAN PROCESSES

Client's Name_____

FOCAL PROBLEMS:

1._____

_____

2._____

_____

3._____

_____

4._____

_____

GOALS AND RELATED OBJECTIVES	ACHIEVED DATE
Abstinence (all psychoactive drugs)	
"Quit Day" achieved	_____
Negative UDS	_____
Commit to Enter Treatment Program	
Understand and agree to program rules	_____
Recognize and accept CD diagnosis	_____
Acknowledge need for help from others	_____
Make child-care, job and other arrangements	_____

Drug-Safe Environment

Drug-free residence _____

Drug-free workplace _____

Drug-free leisure places _____

Dispose of drugs and drug paraphernalia _____

Dispose of drug-related telephone no.s _____

Move residence if necessary _____

Change phone number if necessary _____

Sever drug-using and
   drug-dealing relationships _____

Make the Recovery Commitment

Complete your key commitment step _____

Bonding Involvement With a 12-Step Group

Document attendance at 4 or more
   AA meetings weekly _____

Secure one or more sponsors _____

Actively participate in AA meetings _____

Actively Participate in the Treatment Process

Interact openly and honestly with
   leaders and others _____

Practice the rule of confidentiality _____

Carry out homework assignments _____

Learn and Practice Activity/Time-Use Planning

Keep a daily chart for a clean routine _____

Write a safe time-use plan
   each weekend _____

Identify "Triggers" to Drug Using or Thinking

Plan and practice avoiding
avoidable triggers _____

Recognize and cope with
unavoidable triggers _____

Identify and Develop a Personal Support System

Complete "Supporters/Underminers"
form _____

Share treatment work with family,
friends and others _____

Significant others visit
treatment session _____

Conjoint family counseling
with family members _____

Learn Myths and Facts about Addiction

Recognize and share own
misconceptions re addiction _____

Recognize and share own
denial patterns _____

Learn the Dynamics of Change

Complete the Key to Change checklist _____

Learn the Steps to Change _____

Learn How to Make the Most of Treatment

Recognize ways recovery can be sabotaged _____

Know the ways to treatment success _____

Cope with Episodes of Craving

Learn three ways to stop craving _____

Learn and practice
  Relaxation exercises _____

Learn and practice HALT
  relapse prevention _____

Learn and practice HEDS methods
  to combat craving _____

Know and use 12 more ways
  to counter craving _____

Learn and Understand the Addiction Disease Processes

Know biological/neurological
  aspects of addiction

Know social and behavioral
  aspects of addiction

Other Goals _____

_____

_____

The above goals and objectives have been explained to me and I agree with them.

Client Signature _____

Date _____

Staff Signature _____

Date _____

THREE WAYS TO STOP CRAVING: DEBATE, DISTRACT, DEEP-BREATHE

When you let yourself dwell on the idea of getting high, your heart may start to beat faster in anticipation. The more excited you become, the more your craving is stimulated. If you do not stop this pre-drug upswing early, you may be too late. Probably the most reliable method of stopping the craving is to ask someone supportive to be with you.

But in crises, you can use debating, distracting, and deep-breathing. Debating is a way of thinking through a craving. Distraction works by replacing drug-seeking with other activities and by replacing drug thoughts with thoughts about those activities. Replacing is always a more effective strategy than just removing because it refocuses your attention and offers new motivations. Deep-breathing is a form of meditation that works by slowing you down. You are not likely to be racing toward a high when you are feeling peaceful. But remember that debating, distracting, and deep-breathing all require practice. You will not be able to use the techniques in a crisis unless you practice them on a daily basis. They must already be second nature when thoughts about drugs begin.

DEBATE

Addicts often speak of the "little voice" that tells them to get high. This voice is a natural result of addiction. The recovering person must learn to oppose it with a recovering voice. The recovering voice debates the addict voice and exposes its false arguments. When the addict voice tells you to take drugs to feel better, the recovering voice asks immediately, "But for how long? And then what?" When the

202

addict voice dwells on lost pleasures, the recovering voice speaks of the more solid rewards that drug use prevents. When the addict voice suggests that things might be different this time, the recovering voice should object. You have told yourself that before and deceived yourself. When the addict voice makes getting high sound glamorous, normal, or exciting, the recovering voice should remind you how ugly and sick getting high can be. For every "pro" that the addict voice puts forth, the recovering voice should have a strong list of "cons." But remember that the recovering voice is new and needs strengthening by other positive voices. If you carry on your debate only in solitude, you will start to lose it.

DISTRACT

At the first thought of drug use, do something else. Useful distractions are ones that (a) you enjoy; (b) you can do at any time of the day and in many places; (c) are immediately rewarding (eating a favorite snack); (d) increase self-esteem (working out, doing chores); (e) require some concentration (building a shelf, writing a letter, reading a thriller); (f) are soothing and repetitious (doing the dishes, mopping the floor, folding the laundry); and (g); require energy and reduce tension (running).

DEEP-BREATHE

(1) Find a comfortable position in a quiet room. (2) Let go of muscle tension by contracting and then relaxing deeply each group of muscles (from your feet to your face). (3) Take a deep breath and hold it as long as you can. Let it all out, and imagine that your tensions and drug urges are expelled with it. Feel yourself letting go of harmful attachments and coming to a peaceful place in yourself. Repeat this

ten times. (4)As you let your breath flow in and out, you may begin focusing on a peaceful image, such as moonlight on a lake, or a peaceful word, such as "calm" or "serene." You will notice that all sorts of thoughts keep jumping in. Just let them flow past and keep returning to your image or word until it is your only focus. Notice the slowing of the breath. (After a few weeks of practice, you will be able to slow your breathing and heart rate rather quickly.) You should practice this at least 20 minutes a day.

By Permission: McAuliffe & Albert. (1992). Clean Start. Guilford Press. P. XIX

TREATMENT STAGE I SUMMARY

1. Quit drinking & using. Produce negative drug screens.

   Accept CD diagnosis.

   Engender hope of recovery.

   Commit to enter treatment.

2. Behavior and environmental changes.

   Drug/alcohol safe environment: residence, workplace, places of leisure.

   Sever relations with dealers, drug users, compulsive drinkers.

   Bonding relations with 12-step drug-free group.

   Make recovery commitments.

   Participate actively in treatment process/program.

   Learn and practice time-use planning and structure.

   Identify negative/costly consequences of A&D use.

   Identify "triggers" to drug using, thinking, feelings.

   Learn ways to avoid, stop and/or cope with craving.

   Learn how treatment can succeed or be sabotaged.

   Identify and/or develop a personal support system.

   Learn the biopsychosocial-spiritual view of addiction.

   Learn the myths and facts about addiction.

   Learn the dynamics of change.

   Learn to recognize and take credit for recovery progress.

3. Cognitive and Affective Changes.

   Recognize addictive thinking and feelings.

EFFECTIVE CD COUNSELING

Learn interventions and behaviors to cope with addictive thoughts and feelings.

Use planning tools to structure time around safe relationships and social skills.

Expand understanding and management of own using/drinking triggers.

Use support system resources (counselors, sponsors, family, clergy) to deal with stress, guilt, anger, and other emotional issues.

Practice skills of listening for and questioning new learning to expand healthy living options.

Expand understanding of the disease of addiction.

Expand an understanding of the affective patterns and processes of recovery.

The first phase of recovery and treatment must be the attainment of abstinence. A clean (negative) UDS (urine drug screen) should be seen as an early milestone toward recovery. In many instances the new chemical dependency client may lack the conviction that abstinence is necessary for her. Initial abstinence may require being based on a contractual agreement between the client and the counselor. Achievement of abstinence involves breaking away from the drug and alcohol using scenes and avoiding drug/alcohol using situations. The newcomer to treatment should receive strong support in achieving a drug-free residence, a drug-free workplace, and drug-free places of leisure. Counseling in the time of new abstinence should concentrate heavily upon the necessity for abstinence for successful recovery. Abstinence must be presented as more than a discipline.

The successful client must gain a clear understanding of why the abstinent condition is crucial to recovery, the key to regaining control of her life, a necessity to being teachable, and a foundation for long-term recovery and health. Early brief deviations from abstinence, "slips", are likely to occur. "Slips" are opportunities for teaching, reinforcement of the reasons why abstinence is necessary, why it is difficult to achieve, and why the tools for avoiding relapse must be put to use. Chastisement for brief slips can have negative results, such as teaching others in the group to cover up their own problems as a way of avoiding censure. A chronic relapser should be referred to a more restrictive treatment modality.

A PROGRESSIVE RECOVERY TOUR GUIDE

STAGE I: Intensive Phase (Detox and post-detox).
Short-term goals:

1. Survival of detox and drug withdrawal

2. Daily: abstinence - staying drug free

3. Dealing with crises of withdrawal and post-withdrawal

Give support, encouragement - begin building support
network of people who are accessible to the client in a crisis
(The counselor is warned against taking this role. For the
counselor it means surrendering omnipotence and putting a
priority on her own health - counselors are important, too.
For the client it means an opportunity for growth of survival
skills, self-confidence and a sense of personal responsibility.

Beware of "ownership" of "your" clients. Counselors are
really not indispensable to the client's ultimate recovery.
Teach the client what to expect and how to use available
resources to cope with a crisis).

4. Help the client to learn what are reasonable and realistic
treatment expectations. Debunk the myths and misinformation, teach the nature of the addictive disease, build trust
so the client will allow herself to be led at this point (i.e., to
take some of what she is told on faith until she can see more
clearly), teach the realities of early recovery as they relate
to the nature of the illness and the realities of the individual
client's life situation (personality, social and economic situation, etc.)

The counselor must also be realistic about what to expect.

5. Keep the client in treatment! Seven to ten days post-detox is a critical time for the chemically dependent person in
an inpatient or residential program. It is a period in which

the person vacillates between staying or leaving, while the pain and discomfort of early abstinence struggles to overshadow the pain of continuing to drink or drug.

6. Complete Step 1 of AA program with help and encouragement from the staff.

STAGE II: Intermediate phase. Short-term goals:

1. Staying clean and sober one day at a time.

2. Continue building the support system.

3. Begin developing an aftercare (continuing care) plan.

4. Build defenses against relapse.

5. Continue alcohol and drug education.

6. Complete AA Steps II, III, and IV.

7. Learn or relearn social and leisure management skills.

8. Complete family program with family or significant other.

9. Attend all scheduled in-house AA meetings and frequent community AA meetings.

10. Complete aftercare plan and a crisis plan.

11. Complete Step V of AA program (if ready).

12. Get a self-help group sponsor of the same sex. A temporary sponsor may be necessary at first.

STAGE III: Maintenance. Long-term goals:

1. Establish a "home" AA group and attend it regularly.

2. Attend treatment program's Aftercare group regularly.

3. Become active in program's Alumni Association.

4. Complete Step V of AA program if not done during the intermediate phase.

5. Complete Steps VI through XII of AA program.

6. Activate aftercare plans that involve other community support systems (e.g., family or mental health counseling, financial counseling, etc.).

7. Establish the program and its staff as an open and available resource for use in a crisis, especially one which endangers continuing sobriety and recovery.

Bibliography

AN ANNOTATED LIST OF SELECTED READINGS AND REFERENCED WORKS

Bibliography

ANNOTATED BIBLIOGRAPHY

Alcoholics Anonymous, *Alcoholics Anonymous: The Story of How Many Thousands of Men and Women Have Recovered from Alcoholism.* Alcoholics Anonymous World Services, New York, 3rd. ed., 1976. (Popularly known as The Big Book, this is the basic study book of the AA fellowship).

_____, *Came to Believe.* Alcoholics Anonymous World Services, New York, 1973. (This small volume is about accepting the disease diagnosis).

Berg, I. K., & Miller, S. D., *Working With the Problem Drinker: A Solution Focused Approach.* W. W. Norton, New York, 1992. (Some counseling skills for the Stage I and II treatment counselor).

Blum, K., & Payne, J., *Alcohol and the Addictive Brain: New Hope for Alcoholics from Biogenetic Research.* The Free Press, New York, 1991. (A review of biochemical research related to alcoholism and its importance in treating alcoholism).

Cahalan, D., *Understanding America's Drinking Problem: How to Combat the Hazards of Alcohol*. Jossey-Bass, San Francisco, 1987. (A non-biased account of the history of alcoholism treatment in the United States).

Dyer, W. W., & Vriend, J., *Counseling Techniques That Work*, Funk Wagnalls, New York, 1977. (Helpful counseling strategies, especially for the Stage II treatment counselor).

Goodwin, D. W., *Is Alcoholism Hereditary?* Ballantine Books, New York, 1976. (The author of ground-breaking research in the heritability of alcoholism reviews his and other research and ways the results can be used in the treatment process).

Goulding, R. L. & Mary McC. Goulding, *The Power is in the Patient*. TA Press, San Francisco, 1978. (A TA/Gestalt approach to psychotherapy and a unique method of contracting for change).

Hansen, P. L., *Sick and Tired of Being Sick and Tired*. Graphic Publishing, Lake Mills, Iowa, 1971. A compelling personal account).

Ketcham, K., & Mueller, L. A., *Eating Right to Live Sober*. A Signet Book, New York, 1983. (A guide to the often underplayed aspect of treatment).

Kinney, J., & Leaton, G., *Loosening the Grip: A Handbook of Alcohol Information*, 5th ed. Mosby, St. Louis, 1995. (A great deal of alcoholism lore).

Klein, S. B., *Learning: Principles and Applications*. McGraw-Hill, New York, 1967. (Explains the processes of learning including the phenomenon of state-dependent learning in both animals and humans).

McAuliffe, W. E. & Albert, J., *Clean Start: An Outpatient Program for Initiating Cocaine Recovery*. Guilford Press, New York, 1992. (A highly recommended book for structuring a Stage I Treatment program).

Metzgar, L., *From Denial to Recovery: Counseling Problem Drinkers, Alcoholics, and Their Families*. Jossey-Bass, San Francisco, 1988. (A practical guide to alcoholism counseling and the progressive nature of the disease).

Milam, J. R., & Ketcham, K., *Under the Influence: A Guide to the Myths and Realities of Alcoholism*. Bantam Books, New York, 1981. (A no-nonsense book on the reality of alcoholism, the disease).

Miller, S. N., *Addiction Psychiatry: Current Diagnosis and Treatment*. Wiley-Liss, New York, 1995. (A realistic understanding of addiction and its treatment from the psychiatric profession).

_____, *Treatment of the Addictions: Applications of Outcome Research for Clinical Management*. Harrington Park Press, New York, 1995.

Mooney, A. J., Eisenberg, A., & Eisenberg, H., *The Recovery Book*. Workman Publishing, New York, 1992. (Recommended reading for the   recovering alcoholic; a reference book that touches all the bases).

Mueller, A. L., & Ketcham, K., *Recovering: How to Get and Stay Sober*. Bantam Books, New York, 1987. (A basic book on the stages of the treatment process).

Mumey, J., *The Joy of Being Sober: A Book for Recovering Alcoholics – and Those Who Love Them*. Contemporary Books, Chicago, 1984. (About achieving and enjoying an alcohol-free lifestyle).

Robertson, J., & Monte, T., *Peak Performance Living.* Harper, San Francisco, 1996. (The author describes a program of lifestyle and emotional changes using behaviors and dietary choices to balance neuro-chemistry. Not specifically about treatment of chemical dependence, the book provides numerous suggestions to help construct a new, drug-free lifestyle. A Stage I resource).

Royce, J. E., & Scratchley, D., *Alcoholism and Other Drug Problems.* The Free Press, New York, 1996. (This respected authority on the disease gives his view on the importance of documenting its progression in onset and recovery).

Stewart, I., & Joines, V., TA *Today: A New Introduction to Transactional Analysis.* Lifespace Publishing, Nottingham, England and Chapel Hill, NC, 1987. (Includes a comprehensive coverage of the concept of the drama triangle, its roles of victim, persecutor and rescuer in psychological game playing).

Vaillant, G. E., *The Natural History of Alcoholism: Causes, Patterns, and Paths to Recovery.* Harvard University Press, Cambridge, MA, 1983. (Should be required reading for every professional who works with alcoholics or their families).

Vaughan, C., *Addictive Drinking: The Road to Recovery for Problem Drinkers and Those Who Love Them.* Penguin Books, New York, 1986. (An insightful account of a personal recovery, its successes and its frustrations).

Vaughan, S. C., *The Talking Cure: The Science Behind Psychotherapy.* Grossett/Putnam, New York, 1997. (A readable discourse on the research that supports the physical changes in regions of the brain as the result of psychotherapy and other therapeutic relationships. Recommended for all counselors of Stage II and dual diagnosed chemically dependent clients).

Wallace, J., *Alcoholism: New Light on the Disease.* Edgehill Publications, Newport, RI, 1985. (Excellent material providing a clear explanation of neurological processes in the brain of the alcoholic. Good resource for client education about their disease).

_____, *Writings.* Edgehill Publications, Newport, RI, 1989. (In this book Dr. Wallace covers most aspects of the disease of alcoholism, including a psychological approach to treatment, and upgraded data on disease research).

Wallen, J., *Addiction in Human Development: Developmental Perspectives on Addiction and Recovery.* The Haworth Press, New York, 1993. (An interesting feature of the developmental perspective of the addictive disease is that recovery can result from changes in the effects of trauma and other developmental influences).

Washton, A. M., *Cocaine Addiction: Treatment: Recovery, and Relapse Prevention.* W. W. Norton, New York, 1989. (Without the extensive data from biochemical research currently available, this author perceived the biological vulnerability of the addiction. He also focuses on the need of abstinence from all psychoactive drugs, and the need for delivering treatment progressively. A valuable contribution to chemical dependence treatment literature).

Williams, R. J., *The Prevention of Alcoholism Through Nutrition.* Bantam Books, New York, 1981. (This highly regarded biochemist had a keen interest in alcoholism and sought nutritional means to resist the disease. He seems to have failed in that effort, but his research gave us the principle of the individual differences in metabolism of substances we ingest. This discovery helps to understand why some users of psychoactive drugs become dependent and others do not. There is no standard metabolism).

About the Author

Dr. S. Edmund Hale received his Bachelor of Arts degree in 1950 from the University of Chattanooga; Diploma in Group and Family Therapy in 1979 from Southeast Institute; Master of Education in 1986 from the University of Tennessee at Chattanooga; and his Doctorate of Education in 1994 at the University of Tennessee, Knoxville and Newport University.

In the 1970s Dr. Hale served as Head of Alcohol and Drug Dependency Services and Adult Services Clinician at the Chattanooga Psychiatric Clinic; Executive Director, Chattanooga Council for Alcohol and Drug Abuse Services; and Therapist and Director of Alcohol and Drug Abuse Services at Valley Psychiatric Hospital.

In the 1980s he was Corporate Vice President, Clinical Programs of Greenleaf Health Systems; Senior Counselor and Program Director of program start-up and program development at Crossroads Treatment Center; was a member of the Adjunct Faculty Teaching drugs and drug law to criminal justice majors at University of Tennessee at Chattanooga; and taught substance abuse counseling certificate candidates at Cleveland State Community College.

During the late 1980s and continuing until his "retirement" from private practice in counseling and psychotherapy consultation with Personal Counseling Service in 1999, he continued treating clients having emotional, developmental, behavioral, and personality disorders, and helping clients dealing with chemical dependence and other mental and affective conditions. He was a consultant to mental health clinics and hospitals in chemical dependence treatment, and psychiatric and substance abuse program development. From 1993 through 1996 he was Assistant Professor and Coordinator of Human Services Specialist Degree Program at Cleveland State Community College. He also served as an instructor in counseling and personality theories, counseling techniques, group counseling, substance abuse theory, substance abuse treatment methods, and other subjects.

He is a retired member of the American Counseling Association, Tennessee Counseling Association, American Mental Health Counselors Association, Tennessee Mental Health Counselors Association, and the Lookout Counselors Association. He held professional certification or licenses as TN Certified Substance Abuse Counselor, TN Certified Professional Counselor, TN Licensed Professional Counselor, and TN Mental Heath Services Provider.

STATEMENT FROM THE AUTHOR

Dr. Hale says, "In my CD career I was fortunate to have been heavily involved as developer of program services and programs, and as consultant to numerous CD programs over the southeast, the southwest, and the midwest. These exposures and my own counseling experience have led me to strong convictions that certain elements of Stage I CD treatment are effective and essential. There are also elements being practiced which may be impediments to recovery. *Effective CD Counseling* intends to examine a number of both the positive and negative of these elements."

TO ORDER COPIES of *Effective CD Counseling*, send the information below with a check or money order payable to S. Ed Hale, to 6578 Hickory Meadow Drive, Chattanooga, TN 37421.

Name: _____

Shipping Address: _____

_____

City: _____

St._____ Zip: _____

_____ quantity @ $24.95 = _____

Shipping and handling $3.50 _____

Please include $3.50 for one book. No additional charge for shipping and handling of larger quantities ordered at one time.

— — — — — — — — — — — — — —

TO ORDER COPIES of *Effective CD Counseling*, send the information below with a check or money order payable to S. Ed Hale, to 6578 Hickory Meadow Drive, Chattanooga, TN 37421.

Name: _____

Shipping Address: _____

_____

City: _____

St._____ Zip: _____

_____ quantity @ $24.95 = _____

Shipping and handling $3.50 _____

Please include $3.50 for one book. No additional charge for shipping and handling of larger quantities ordered at one time.

Goudy Old Style on BVG 50# digital white
Type and design by Karen Stone